AN INTRODUCTION TO THE

BIBLE

AN INTRODUCTION TO THE

BIBLE

JENNY ROBERTS

SHOOTING STAR PRESS

A QUANTUM BOOK

Published by Shooting Star Press, Inc.
230 Fifth Avenue, Suite 1212
New York, NY 10001
USA

ISBN 1-57335-521-6

This book was produced by
Quantum Books Ltd
6 Blundell Street
London N7 9BH

Printed in China by Leefung-Asco Printers Ltd

Contents

MAPS AND CHARTS

Order and Abbreviations of Books of the Bible

OLD TESTAMENT			
	ABBREVIATION		**ABBREVIATION**
GENESIS	GEN.	ECCLESIASTES	ECCLES.
EXODUS	EXOD.	SONG OF SOLOMON	S. OF S.
LEVITICUS	LEV.	ISAIAH	ISA.
NUMBERS	NUM.	JEREMIAH	JER.
DEUTERONOMY	DEUT.	LAMENTATIONS	LAM.
JOSHUA	JOSH.	EZEKIEL	EZEK.
JUDGES	JUDG.	DANIEL	DAN.
RUTH	RUTH	HOSEA	HOS.
1 SAMUEL	1 SAM.	JOEL	JOEL
2 SAMUEL	2 SAM.	AMOS	AMOS
1 KINGS	1 KGS.	OBADIAH	OBAD.
2 KINGS	2 KGS.	JONAH	JONAH
1 CHRONICLES	1 CHR.	MICAH	MIC.
2 CHRONICLES	2 CHR.	NAHUM	NAHUM
EZRA	EZRA	HABAKKUK	HAB.
NEHEMIAH	NEH.	ZEPHANIAH	ZEPH.
ESTHER	ESTHER	HAGGAI	HAG.
JOB	JOB	ZECHARIAH	ZECH.
PSALMS	PS.	MALACHI	MAL.
PROVERBS	PROV.		

NEW TESTAMENT			
	ABBREVIATION		**ABBREVIATION**
MATTHEW	MATT.	1 TIMOTHY	1 TIM.
MARK	MARK	2 TIMOTHY	2 TIM.
LUKE	LUKE	TITUS	TITUS
JOHN	JOHN	PHILEMON	PHILEM.
ACTS	ACTS	HEBREWS	HEB.
ROMANS	ROM.	JAMES	JAS.
1 CORINTHIANS	1 COR.	1 PETER	1 PET.
2 CORINTHIANS	2 COR.	2 PETER	2 PET.
GALATIANS	GAL.	1 JOHN	1 JOHN
EPHESIANS	EPH.	2 JOHN	2 JOHN
PHILIPPIANS	PHIL.	3 JOHN	3 JOHN
COLOSSIANS	COL.	JUDE	JUDE
1 THESSALONIANS	1 THESS.	REVELATION	REV.
2 THESSALONIANS	2 THESS.		

Introduction

HE WORD 'BIBLE' comes, through Latin, from the Greek word biblia, *meaning 'books', which in its turn comes from* byblos, *meaning 'papyrus', the material from which books were made.*

THE TEXTS

We are used to speaking of the Bible as 'a book', but in fact it is a collection of books, of different authorship and written at different times, which have been selected from a wider range of writings to make up the Bible as we know it. The books of the Old Testament were written over centuries and some of them were added to or changed their form over many years. None of the original manuscripts have survived, but by the second century BC the Old Testament manuscripts had been organized into the 24 books that make up the Hebrew Bible.

The earliest translation of the Hebrew scriptures was the Septuagint, a translation into Greek of all the Old Testament canonical books, and some of those that are regarded by many as apocryphal. The Jewish translators (traditionally 72 of them) started work on the Pentateuch (Genesis, Exodus, Leviticus, Numbers and Deuteronomy) in Alexandria in the first half of the third century BC. The other canonical books appear to have been translated by the end of the second century BC. The Septuagint was the basis for several subsequent translations. In AD 382 St Jerome made a Latin translation, called the Vulgate, which is still used by the Roman Catholic Church.

Where translations of the Old Testament books are taken from the Hebrew, the source is generally what is known as the Masoretic text or Masora. The Masoretes (transmitters) probably started their work in about AD 500 and did not finish it until the 10th century.

Most biblical texts have come down to us as a result of repeated copying in a perishable medium such as leather or papyrus. This can give rise to doubts about the historical authenticity of the texts. The greatest archaeological breakthrough in this area has undoubtedly been the discovery of the Dead Sea Scrolls in 1947. The Scrolls were discovered in a cave near the Dead Sea and finally

RIGHT: One of the Qumran Caves, just north-west of the Dead Sea, where the oldest existing Bible manuscripts were found. The scrolls were discovered by chance in 1947 when a shepherd came across a cave in the cliff face and found inside some old pottery jars containing bundles of cloth wrapped round rolls of leather. Their identity was eventually confirmed by the American scholar John Trever. Fragments of every canonical Old Testament book, except the Book of Esther, were present, and the manuscripts date from the last few centuries BC to the beginning of the first century AD.

LEFT: Part of the Isaiah Scroll, the first of the Dead Sea Scrolls to be identified. The book of Isaiah consisted of a roll of leather 61 cm (2 ft) long, and made up of 17 sheets sewn together. It was covered with 54 columns of Hebrew script. The illustration shows the last columns of the scroll, covering Isaiah 65:4 to 66:24.

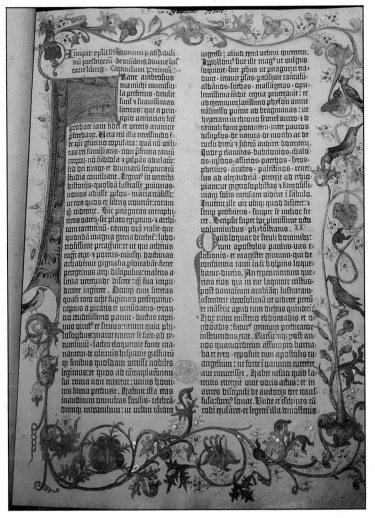

These were not so much translations as poetical works of paraphrase, and no manuscripts have been found. During the later Middle English period various parts of the Bible were translated, but the most significant work was that associated with John Wycliffe (1320–1384), a reformer whose aim was to make the scriptures accessible to the people.

Although Bibles were being printed in Europe from the middle of the fifteenth century, it was not until 1525 that the first Bible to be printed in English appeared. This was the Tyndale Bible, produced by William Tyndale, a scholar who, like Wycliffe, was determined to make the Bible more available to ordinary lay people. It was significant not just as the first printed English Bible, but as the first to be translated from the Greek, rather than Latin. In 1536 Tyndale was arrested for heresy and executed. Tyndale's translation has been enormously influential, and much of his work is preserved in the English of the King James Version.

The sixteenth century saw the publication of several significant English translations. Miles Coverdale's translation was published in 1535, and was taken partly from the Vulgate, partly from German versions, and partly from Tyndale. His was the first Bible in which noncanonical books were published under the separate heading of 'Apocrypha'.

In 1537 the English version known as Matthew's Bible appeared and two years later the Taverner Bible, a revision of Matthew's Bible, was published. Another very influential work appeared in 1539: the Great Bible, so called because of its large size. This was prepared by Miles Coverdale and was authorized by Archbishop Cranmer for distribution in all churches and to all people.

Under Mary Tudor, Protestants were persecuted and Bibles were taken from churches. Many Protestants fled from England, and a group of them who went to Geneva began to produce a Bible there. The Geneva Bible was based on the Great Bible but with attention paid to Hebrew scholarship, and was the first Bible where the chapters were divided into verses. When Elizabeth took over the throne, England became safe again, but the work continued to be centred in Geneva. It appeared in 1560 but did not receive official endorsement. Instead the current Archbishop of Canterbury ordered a revision of the work, the Bishops' Bible, which appeared in 1568, with a revised version in 1572. This revised version was to be the basis for the King James Version.

ABOVE: A page from the Gutenberg Bible, which was printed in Mainz in Germany in 1455. This was the first Bible ever printed and was also the first large book to be printed from moveable metal type.

OPPOSITE: The first page of Luke's Gospel from the Lindisfarne Gospels. This beautifully ornamented manuscript comes from Northumbria, England, and dates from about AD 700. It was written in Latin but an English gloss, or interlinear translation, was added in about AD 950.

identified as Hebrew texts. One of them was a copy of the book of Isaiah, which turned out to be around 1,000 years older than any existing Hebrew manuscript. When compared with the Masoretic texts, various differences were found but on the whole there were no major changes, and the discovery tended to give greater authority to the accuracy of the Jewish copyists.

The books of the New Testament were written, in Greek, during the first century AD, but the earliest manuscripts date from the third and fourth centuries AD. There are about 175 manuscripts dating from this period, written on papyrus or parchment, most of them very well preserved.

THE BIBLE IN ENGLISH

The first attempts at translating parts of the Bible into English began in the seventh century AD.

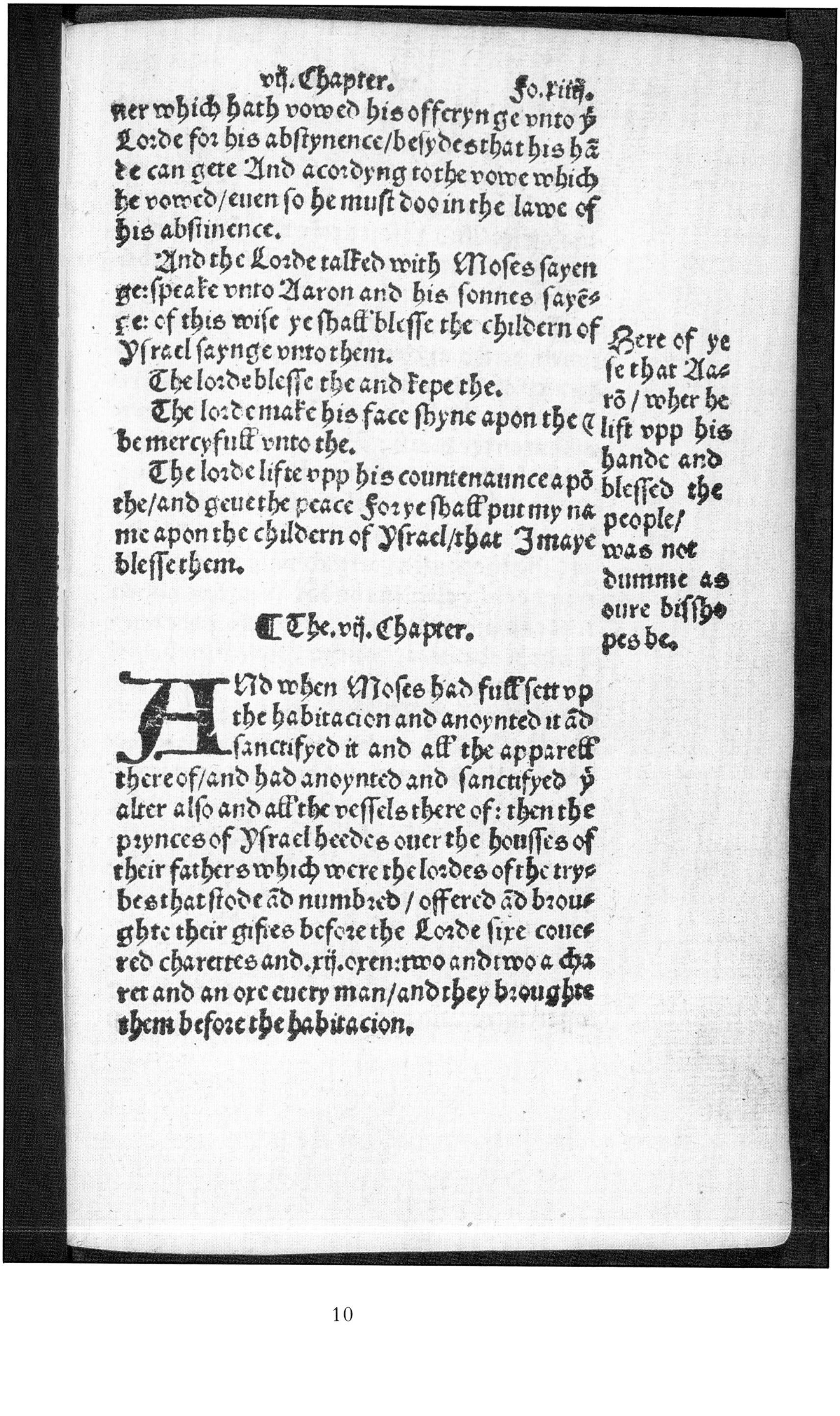

vij. Chapter.　　　　fo. riiij.

ner which hath vowed his offerynge vnto ÿ
Lorde for his abstynence/besydes that his hã
de can gete And acordyng to the vowe which
he vowed/euen so he must doo in the lawe of
his abstinence.

And the Lorde talked with Moses sayen
ge: speake vnto Aaron and his sonnes saye
ge: of this wise ye shall blesse the childern of
Ysrael saynge vnto them.

The lorde blesse the and kepe the.

The lorde make his face shyne apon the ã
be mercyfull vnto the.

The lorde lifte vpp his countenaunce apõ
the/and geue the peace for ye shall put my na
me apon the childern of Ysrael/that I maye
blesse them.

Here of ye
se that Aa
rõ / wher he
lift vpp his
hande and
blessed the
people/
was not
dumme as
oure bissho
pes be.

The. vij. Chapter.

And when Moses had full sett vp
the habitacion and anoynted it ãd
sanctifyed it and all the apparell
thereof/and had anoynted and sanctifyed ÿ
alter also and all the vessels there of: then the
prynces of Ysrael heedes ouer the housses of
their fathers which were the lordes of the try
bes that stode ãd numbred / offered ãd brou
ghte their giftes before the Lorde sixe coue
red charettes and.rij. oxen: two and two a cha
ret and an oxe euery man/and they broughte
them before the habitacion.

RIGHT: Part of
the book of Numbers,
from the sixteenth-
century Tyndale Bible.

The Authorized or King James Version was commissioned by James I. Work started on it in 1604 and it was printed in 1611. The basis for the translation was the Bishops' Bible but the translators consulted the Greek and Hebrew texts, and followed Tyndale, Matthew, Coverdale, or the Geneva version when it seemed to them that the translation was more accurate. The King James Bible became the standard version for Protestants all over the English-speaking world. It is still much used today, and nearly all modern translations are indebted to it.

In 1870 work on a Revised Version of the King James was started, organized by the Church of England but involving other denominations and American Bible scholars. The complete work was published in 1885 in England, with the American Standard Version published six years later.

Some twentieth-century versions which deserve mention include the Revised Standard Version of 1952, the Roman Catholic Jerusalem Bible of 1966, the New International Bible of 1978, and the best-selling and very popular modern version, the Good News Bible of 1976.

WHY READ THE BIBLE?

The Bible is the best selling and most widely distributed book in the world. In 1988 the United Bible Society reported that the number of languages and dialects into which complete books of the Bible had been translated had reached 1,907. This includes complete Bibles in 310 languages and New Testaments in 695 languages.

Why has the Bible, a collection of ancient and diverse writings, achieved such a status in the modern world? There is no single answer, just as there is no single attitude to the Bible. To some it is the supreme holy book, the inspired word of God, still relevant as a guide to faith and conduct. To others it is primarily a work of great historical interest, charting the history of the Jewish people over centuries, and the origins and growth of the Christian Church. To others it is essentially myth, a collection of stories that evolved to explain natural phenomena and events.

For many people, though, the Bible has no particular significance. It is a book that they own but never read, believing it to be of little interest or relevance. Such people are missing out on a wealth of information and entertainment. Whatever the reader's religious views, the Bible remains an important record of ancient history and ideas, whose influence on Western language and thought is incalculable. It is also a considerable work of literature, containing some beautiful poetry, and many exciting narratives and memorable characters. It has not been possible to include anything like all the fascinating Bible narratives here, and it is hoped that the stories and facts related in this book might send its readers back to the original work with renewed interest.

All quotations in this book are taken from the King James Version. Although subsequent translations have improved on the accuracy of the translation and comprehensibility of the language, the King James is still arguably the most beautifully written and the most memorable of all English Bibles.

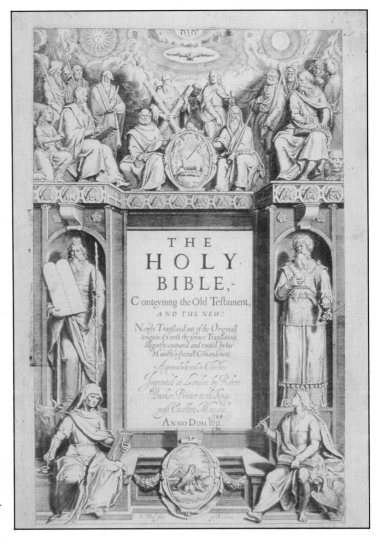

ABOVE: The King James Bible, or the Authorized Version, became the standard work for Protestants and is still widely used. It was printed in 1611, but the first edition was marred by many typographical errors. These were corrected in subsequent editions, which have also modernized spelling and punctuation. Most of the widely-known Bible quotations use the King James version, which is notable for the beauty and force of its language. The illustration shows the title page.

11

In the Beginning

ABOVE: The second chapter of Genesis describes God
bringing all the animals to Adam for him to name. This
hand-tinted illustration comes from an 1816 edition of
the John Brown Bible, which was first printed in 1778.

HE BOOK OF *Genesis, the first book of the Bible, was traditionally believed to have been written by Moses. It is now thought to be a work of composite authorship, written at various times, although much of it probably dates from no later than the time of Moses.*

The early chapters of the book, chapters 1–11, cover the prehistory. Here we have the account of the creation of the world and God's dealings with the first people. The remainder of the book, chapters 12–50, tells the history of the patriarchs: Abraham, Isaac, Jacob and Joseph.

THE CREATION
(Gen. 1–4)

The first three verses of the first book of the Old Testament are some of the best known, and most dramatic, words in the whole Bible. 'In the beginning God created the heaven and the earth. And the earth was without form, and void; and darkness was upon the face of the deep. And the spirit of God moved upon the face of the waters. And God said, Let there be light; and there was light.'

The first two chapters of Genesis provide slightly differing accounts of the order in which the Creation proceeded. According to chapter 1, on the first five days, God created day and night; heaven and earth; the seas, and all the plant life; the sun, moon, and stars; and all the animals, birds, and fishes. On the sixth, 'God created man in his own image . . . male and female created he them' and they were given the charge over the earth and all the living things that God had made. Chapter 2 describes God forming Adam out of the dust of the ground, and placing him in the garden of Eden. God then formed all the animals out of the ground, and each was brought to Adam to name. Finally, God sent Adam into a deep sleep and removed one of his ribs. Out of this he formed a woman, Eve, to be Adam's companion.

ADAM AND EVE

Adam was given the task of tending the garden, and God told him that he could eat from any tree in the garden except for one – the tree of the knowledge of good and evil – and apparently Adam passed on this instruction to his wife. But the serpent set out to tempt Eve. He questioned her about God's instructions, and she told him that God had said that they would die if they ate from the forbidden tree. The serpent persuaded

LEFT: This engraving by Badalocchio (1581-1647) illustrates Genesis 1:4: '. . . and God divided the light from the darkness'.

her that this was untrue and that eating this fruit would give them the wisdom of gods.

Eve could not resist the serpent's wiles. She took one of the fruits and gave one to Adam, and they both ate. The immediate result of their disobedience was that they experienced shame. They had been happily naked up until then, but suddenly became aware of their nakedness and embarrassed by it; they sewed fig leaves together to cover themselves. Then they heard God walking in the garden and they hid from him.

God discovered them and charged them with disobeying his commands. Adam blamed Eve, and Eve blamed the serpent, but they were cast out of Eden. Their disobedience brought the punishment of hard work for men, painful childbearing for women, and eventual death for all

CAIN AND ABEL

After the expulsion from Eden, Eve became pregnant and bore a son, Cain. Her second child was also a son, Abel. Cain became a farmer of crops and Abel became a shepherd.

Both Cain and Abel brought an offering to God of their first fruits: the new crops and the first lamb respectively. God accepted Abel's offering but rejected Cain's. Cain was angry and resentful, and when he and Abel were alone in the fields, he murdered his brother. God called Cain, asking him where Abel was, and Cain made his famous reply, 'I know not: Am I my brother's keeper?'

Cain's punishment was to be driven out and to become a fugitive. But God did not want Cain killed. He set a mark on him so that nobody should kill him, and Cain went to live in the land of Nod.

ABOVE: As a punishment for their disobedience, Adam and Eve were cast out of the Garden of Eden. This illustration of the expulsion from Eden is a detail from a nineteenth-century window in the Church of St Aignan at Chartres, France.

LEFT: The first murder: Cain's slaying of his brother Abel. The engraving is by the Dutch artist Lucas van Leyden (c 1494-1533).

ABOVE: There is a
wealth of detail in this
delightful painting of *The
Animals Entering Noah's
Ark* by Jacob Savery II
(1593-1627).

At the time of Noah, confusion, violence and wickedness was reigning, for there had been inter-marriage between humankind and supernatural beings. God saw this sinfulness, and he regretted having created the human race. He decided to destroy his creation, not only people, but every living creature he had made.

However, amongst all this sin and corruption, God recognized that there was one just and godly man, Noah, and decided that he would save him and his family. He gave Noah instructions for building an ark from gopher wood. He was to enter it with his family, and take on board male and female pairs of every animal and bird, besides supplies of food.

Noah built the ark, and entered it, as God had instructed. Then for 40 days and nights it rained without ceasing. The waters lifted up the ark, which continued to float as the flood increased. The flood persisted for 150 days, and every living thing was consumed by it, apart from Noah, his family, and the animals in the ark.

Eventually the flood abated, and the ark came to rest on the top of the mountains of Ararat. Noah sent out a dove as a messenger, and when it returned carrying an olive leaf, he knew that the flood was over. When he emerged from the ark, Noah built an altar to God, who blessed him, promising never to destroy creation in the same way again. God placed a rainbow in the sky as a sign of his covenant with Noah.

ABOVE: An illustration from an 1816 edition of the John Brown Bible, showing Noah and his sons greeting the rainbow, the sign of God's covenant with them (Gen. 9:1-17).

THE FLOOD
(Gen. 5–9)

Adam and Eve had a third son, Seth, and chapter 5 records the extraordinary longevity of the dynasty that started with Adam, with the record set by Methuselah, who is said to have lived to the age of 969. The last of the dynasty recorded here was Noah, who had three sons, Shem, Ham and Japheth.

BUILDING OF THE TOWER OF BABEL
GENESIS XI

LONDON, THOMAS KELLY

ABOVE: Although archaeologists and explorers have long searched Babylon for the remains of the Tower of Babel, it has never been found. This illustration of the Tower is from the John Brown Bible.

THE TOWER OF BABEL
(Gen. 11)

In those days there was only one language spoken in the earth.

The people travelled eastwards until they came to the plain of Shinar (Sumer in ancient Babylonia), where they settled and began to build a city. Then they embarked upon the building of a great tower, whose top was to reach heaven. God saw what they were doing and punished their pride by bringing about a confusion of their speech, so that they all spoke different languages and could not understand each other. As a result the people became scattered abroad, all over the earth, and the city became known as Babel (actually from Assyrian *bāb-ilu* meaning 'gate of God' but associated in popular etymology with Hebrew *bālal* meaning 'confusion').

ABRAHAM AND ISAAC
(Gen. 11–25)

One of the descendants of Noah's son Shem was a godly and wealthy man called Abram. He lived with his wife Sarai and nephew Lot in Ur in Babylonia, but God instructed him to leave that place and travel south, promising that if he obeyed he would become the father of a great nation. Eventually they came to Canaan, where they separated, Abram remaining in Canaan, and Lot travelling on to Sodom.

HAGAR AND ISHMAEL

Sarai was barren, so she urged Abram to try to father a child on her Egyptian handmaid Hagar. Hagar became pregnant and, as a result, began to act in a contemptuous way towards her mistress. Sarai responded by treating Hagar harshly and, unable to tolerate this, Hagar fled from her. But

LEFT: This fourteenth-century French manuscript illustration shows God's covenant with Abraham.

an angel met her and persuaded her to return, telling her that she would have a son who would be called Ishmael, a wild man who would be alienated from everybody. She returned and eventually gave birth to Ishmael.

GOD'S COVENANT WITH ABRAHAM

When Abram was 99 years old, God appeared to him and renewed his promise that he would make Abram the father of many nations, and would give the land of Canaan to him and his descendants for ever. The sign of the covenant was to be that every male child was to be circumcised at the age of eight days. God changed Abram's name to Abraham (meaning 'father of a multitude'). He told him that Sarai's name was to be changed to Sarah (meaning 'princess') for she was to become the mother of a nation of kings. Abraham laughed at the idea of his elderly barren wife conceiving, but God told him that she would bear a son who would be called Isaac.

The promise that Sarah would have a child was confirmed by three angels who visited Abraham and Sarah and were entertained by them. Like Abraham, Sarah laughed when she heard the promise, but the Lord told Abraham that nothing was too hard for him.

19

LOT AND THE DESTRUCTION OF SODOM

The city of Sodom, where Abraham's nephew Lot had settled, was notorious for wickedness, as was the neighbouring city of Gomorrah. The Lord told Abraham that he was planning the destruction of Sodom, but Abraham pleaded with him not to destroy it if there were any just and innocent people living there.

God sent two angels to Sodom, and Lot entertained them in his house. The men of Sodom created a disturbance outside the house, calling Lot to let his guests out so that they could have sex with them. Lot refused, unwilling to violate the principles of hospitality; however, his high principles did not apparently extend to his own daughters, for he offered them to the men instead. The men of Sodom were about to break the door down when the angel guests intervened. They struck the beseiging men with blindness, and then took Lot, his wife and his daughters away from the city, telling them not to look backward. Once Lot was out of danger God destroyed both Sodom and Gomorrah with fire and brimstone. But Lot's wife looked back, and she was instantly turned into a pillar of salt.

Lot and his daughters went off into the hills and lived in a cave. The daughters' betrothed husbands had perished in the destruction of Sodom and the two young women were afraid that they would not find men in this isolated place and would never have children. So they made their father drunk and both in turn had intercourse with him. Lot was too drunk to know that this had happened but both his daughters conceived and later bore sons. These sons, Moab and Benammi, became the ancestors of the Moabites and the Ammonites, two of the traditional enemies of the Israelites.

ISAAC AND ISHMAEL

As God had promised, Sarah became pregnant in her old age and bore a son, Isaac. At the feast given when Isaac was weaned, Sarah saw the boy Ishmael mocking her son. She begged Abraham to cast out Ishmael and his mother Hagar, for she did not want Isaac to share his inheritance with Ishmael. Abraham was distressed but God told him that he should do what Sarah asked, so he gave Hagar food and water and sent her and their son away.

Hagar and Ishmael wandered in the wilderness of Beersheba until at last all their water had gone. Then Hagar left her son and went off to weep, for she could not bear to witness the death of her child. But God spoke to Hagar, comforting her, and she saw that there was a well in front of her. She took water and gave it to Ishmael. Ishmael grew and prospered, becoming a skilful hunter.

ABOVE: *Lot and his Daughters* by the French painter Simon Vouet (1590–1649) shows Lot's daughters seducing their drunken father.

THE TRIAL OF ABRAHAM'S FAITH

A WIFE FOR ISAAC

Sarah died, and Abraham became concerned about finding a wife for Isaac. He did not want him to marry a Canaanite woman, but wanted a daughter-in-law from his own people in Mesopotamia. He called his most trusted servant and told him to go to that country and try to find a suitable woman to bring back as a wife for Isaac.

The servant took 10 camels and travelled to northern Mesopotamia. He took his camels to the well where the women of the city came to draw water. He then asked God to arrange things so that the first young woman to offer water to him and his camels should be Isaac's designated wife. Before he had even finished praying, a beautiful young woman appeared at the well, and she offered water to the servant, and drew water for his camels.

Abraham's servant asked the girl who she was, and she told him that she was called Rebekah, and was the daughter of Bethuel. This made her Isaac's cousin. She offered him hospitality and he came to the house where she lived with her parents and brother Laban. The family accepted that this marriage was God's will and the servant left for Canaan with Rebekah. Isaac and Rebekah married, and Isaac's love for his wife comforted him for the loss of his mother.

JACOB
(Gen. 26–36)

For the first 20 years of their marriage, Isaac and Rebekah had no children. Isaac prayed to God for his wife, and at last she became pregnant. God told Rebekah that there were two nations in her womb, and the younger would be the stronger.

JACOB AND ESAU

Rebekah gave birth to twins. The first to emerge was red and hairy, and they called him Esau (meaning 'hairy'). The second boy came out holding on to the heel of his brother, and he was called Jacob (similar to Hebrew for 'heel' but also meaning 'supplanter').

The twins grew up, and Esau became a hunter, an outdoors man and his father's favourite. The quieter brother, Jacob, was Rebekah's favourite. One day Esau came back from a hunting expedition, faint with hunger, to find his brother making a stew of red lentils. He begged Jacob to give him some of the stew, but Jacob asked him to give him his birthright (the rights of the first-born son) in

ABRAHAM AND ISAAC

Some time after this, God spoke to Abraham. He told him to take his son Isaac to the mountains and sacrifice him as a burnt offering. Abraham did as God had commanded, taking the boy, and wood for the sacrificial fire.

As they neared the mountains, Isaac asked his father where the lamb for the offering was, and Abraham replied, 'My son, God will provide himself a lamb for the burnt offering'. When they came to the place God had spoken of, Abraham built an altar and laid wood on it. Then he bound Isaac and laid him on the altar. As he raised his knife to kill his son, God called him and told him to stop. For Abraham had proved his faith, and Isaac's life would be spared. Then Abraham saw that a ram was caught in the thicket by its horns, so he took the ram and sacrificed it upon the altar in place of his son.

ABOVE: In this illustration from an 1816 edition of the John Brown Bible, Abraham is arrested in the act of sacrificing his son Isaac by the appearance of a ram in the thicket, God's substitute for the burnt offering.

return. Esau agreed. The people who descended from Esau became known as the Edomites, because of the red lentils (Edom sounds like the Hebrew for 'red').

Isaac became old and nearly blind. He called Esau and asked him to go out hunting and then to cook the game for him in the way he liked best, after which Esau would have his blessing. Rebekah overheard this conversation and when Esau had left for the fields, she told Jacob to kill two young goats for her to cook for Isaac, so that Jacob could receive the blessing instead of him. Jacob pointed out that Esau was a hairy man, whereas he was smooth, and that their father might detect the difference by touch. Rebekah's solution was to cover Jacob's hands and neck with the skin of the goats she had cooked, so that he felt hairy.

Jacob took the meat to his father, saying he was Esau and bidding him to eat and then bless him. Isaac was surprised that it had taken such a short time to kill and cook an animal, but Jacob explained that God had intervened in his hunting. Isaac was puzzled, for the voice that he heard was like Jacob's, but he was reassured that it was Esau when he felt the hairy animal skin. He ate the meat and then blessed his son, asking God to give him prosperity and lordship over all his kin.

Esau had returned from hunting, and had cooked the meat he had caught, and he now appeared, bringing the meal for his father. When he heard Esau's voice Isaac was confused, and gradually both he and Esau realized the deception that had taken place. Esau was distraught and begged his father to bless him too, but Jacob had already been given an older son's blessing, so Isaac could only prophesy that Esau would eventually break away from his brother's dominion over him.

JACOB'S LADDER

Esau was furious with Jacob and was ready to kill him, so Rebekah advised Jacob to go to stay with her brother, Laban. Jacob set off and stopped for the night at a town called Luz, where he slept out in the open, with stones for his pillow.

As he slept, he had a dream in which he saw a ladder reaching to heaven, and angels ascending and descending it. Jacob saw God above the ladder, saying to him that he would give him the land on which he was lying, and he would bless him in all he did, and bless his descendants.

Jacob woke and he set his stone pillows up into a memorial, pouring oil on them and dedicating the pillar to God. He renamed the place Bethel, meaning 'house of God'.

RACHEL AND LEAH

Jacob continued on his journey and came to a well, where there were people watering their flocks. He enquired whether they knew Laban, and was told that his daughter Rachel was just approaching to water her father's sheep. Jacob greeted Rachel with a kiss, telling her that he was her cousin.

Laban welcomed Jacob into his house and he stayed with his uncle, serving him. Laban had two daughters, the beautiful Rachel and her elder sister Leah, and soon Jacob had fallen in love with the younger sister. After a month, Laban asked Jacob what wages he required, and he promised his uncle that he would serve him for another seven years if he could marry Rachel at the end of that time.

When the seven years had passed, Jacob asked Laban for his bride. Laban made a wedding feast, but that night he sent Leah, not Rachel, to Jacob. Brides were normally veiled, and perhaps also Jacob had wined and dined too well at the feast. At any rate, he failed to notice until the morning that he had been tricked. When he remonstrated with Laban, his uncle replied that it was not customary for the younger girl to be married before the older. But he agreed that Jacob could have

Rachel as well as Leah, if he agreed to serve Laban for another seven years.

Jacob married Rachel, and he continued to love her far more than he did her sister. But Rachel was still jealous of her sister, because Leah had had four sons (Reuben, Simeon, Levi and Judah), whereas she herself had not been able to conceive. She gave Jacob her handmaid, Bilhah, so that she could bear Jacob's sons for her, and Bilhah subsequently bore two sons, Dan and Naphtali. Not to be outdone, Leah gave Jacob her maid, Zilpah, who also bore him two sons, Gad and Asher.

Leah's oldest son, Reuben, went into the fields and found mandrakes, which he gave to his mother. Mandrakes were believed to have the ability to produce fertility. When Rachel saw the plants she pleaded with her sister to let her have them, but Leah, jealous of Jacob's love for Rachel, refused. Rachel finally worked out a bargain by which she would have the mandrakes and Leah in return could sleep with Jacob that night instead of her. Leah agreed, and so conceived a fifth son, Issachar. Leah was to have another son, Zebulun and a daughter, Dinah, but Rachel too conceived at last and had a son, Joseph.

25

LEFT: An engraving showing Jacob wrestling with the angel, who dislocated his hip and renamed him Israel (Gen. 32: 24–32).

JACOB MEETS ESAU

Eventually, Jacob and his wives decided that it was time for them to return to Canaan. As they journeyed homeward, Jacob sent messengers to Esau to tell him that he had left Laban and was returning to his country. The messengers returned to say that Esau was on his way with 400 men. Jacob was afraid that his brother had hostile intentions, so he picked out a choice selection from his flocks as a present for Esau and sent servants ahead with them.

While waiting to meet Esau, Jacob sent his party across the River Jabbok, but stayed alone on the other side. An angel appeared and proceeded to wrestle with Jacob all night, until he put Jacob's hip out of joint. Jacob held on to him, and the stranger bade him let him go, for daylight was coming. Jacob said he would not let him go unless he blessed him. The angel then blessed Jacob, calling him 'Israel' (which sounds like the Hebrew for 'he struggles with God').

When Jacob saw Esau approaching at last, he bowed to the ground, hoping to placate him. But Esau ran towards him and hugged him. He too had all he needed and had no ill will towards his brother now. Jacob had to persuade him to accept the gift he had given him, and there was complete reconciliation between the brothers.

26

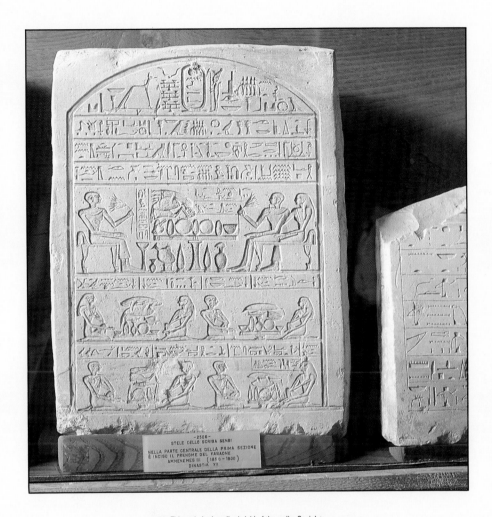

This stela (or inscribed slab) of the scribe Seni dates
from the twelfth dynasty in Egypt, the end of the Middle
Kingdom. In the central part of the upper section is the
name of the Pharaoh Ammenemes III (1850–1800 BC).
This period of Egyptian history predates the oppression
of the Israelite people in Egypt, which started after
Joseph established his family there.

JOSEPH
(Gen. 37–50)

Jacob settled in Canaan with his 12 sons. The last
of these was Rachel's son Benjamin, whose birth
had caused his mother's death. Joseph was Jacob's
favourite, and he made him a decorated robe,
which caused much jealousy and resentment
among his brothers. This increased when Joseph
began to have dreams which indicated that he
would take precedence over all of them.

JOSEPH SOLD INTO EGYPT

One day Jacob sent Joseph to check on his brothers
who were looking after the flocks. As Joseph
approached, his brothers saw him from a distance,
and started to plot how they could get rid of him.
They were going to kill him and throw his body
into a dry well, but Reuben said that they should
throw him into the well alive. He actually planned
to come back and rescue Joseph.

When Joseph arrived, he was thrown into the
well. Just then a party of merchants appeared,

27

travelling to Egypt. Judah suggested that they might sell Joseph to these traders, in that way both avoiding bloodshed and making a profit. This was done and to cover up their crime, the brothers killed a goat, and dipped Joseph's coat in the blood. Then they took the coat to their father who assumed that Joseph had been killed by wild animals. Jacob was distraught with grief and could not be comforted.

JOSEPH AND POTIPHAR'S WIFE

Meanwhile, Joseph had been taken to Egypt and sold there to Potiphar, one of the pharaoh's officials. God blessed everything that Joseph did, and he became Potiphar's most valued servant, taking charge of the running of the household.

Joseph was a good-looking young man, and Potiphar's wife was attracted to him, and began to proposition him. Although she pestered him constantly, Joseph resisted her advances, telling her that

ABOVE: *Joseph Being Sold by his Brothers* by Friedrich Overbeck (1789–1869). Joseph is being taken away by the merchants who will carry him into Egypt. Some of his brothers take the money, while others dip his coat in goat's blood to deceive their father.

Potiphar trusted him and that he could not behave in such an immoral and disloyal way. But one day Potiphar's wife found him alone in the house. She caught him by his robe, but Joseph escaped and ran off, leaving her clutching his robe. Furious, she called the servants and claimed that Joseph had tried to rape her but had run away when she had screamed, leaving his robe behind. When Potiphar came home she told him the same story; he believed her and had Joseph arrested and put in prison.

JOSEPH IN PRISON

Joseph flourished in prison, as he had in Potiphar's house. The jailor soon came to trust him, and left much of the running of the prison to him. After a while Pharaoh's chief butler and baker were both sent to prison. Both of them were troubled by strange dreams, which Joseph was able to interpret. The butler's dream meant that in three days he would be pardoned and restored to his former position, but the baker's meant that in three days

he would be executed. Joseph asked the butler to remember him after he had been released, and to mention him to his master. In three days the butler and baker were both taken from the prison and, as Joseph had predicted, the baker was executed but the butler pardoned. However, the butler forgot all about Joseph.

After two years had passed, Pharaoh was woken one night by a dream. He saw seven fat cows feeding, and then seven thin cows came and ate the fat cows. He slept again and dreamed of seven full ears of corn which were devoured by seven thin ears of corn. In the morning, Pharaoh sent for all his wise men and magicians, but no one could interpret the dreams.

Then the butler suddenly remembered Joseph. He told his master that when he and the baker had been in prison two years before, a young Hebrew

there had been able to interpret their dreams. Joseph was sent for immediately, and Pharaoh told him his dreams. Joseph said that the seven fat cows and ears of corn meant that there would be seven years of plenty. The seven thin cows and ears signified seven years of famine, which would destroy the country. He advised Pharaoh to collect and store a proportion of the food harvested in the seven good years, against the time of famine.

Pharaoh was impressed by Joseph's wisdom. He released him from prison, and put him in charge of the storing of food against the famine. Joseph was now governor over Egypt, second only to the king in authority and wealth.

JOSEPH AND HIS BROTHERS
Under Joseph's governorship, food was stored in the seven good years, and when the famine hit Egypt, the people could be fed. However, the famine had also struck all the surrounding countries, and they had no food stored. When it was known that there was corn available in Egypt, people came from every country hoping to buy food there, and they were brought before Joseph.

Jacob's family were also suffering from the famine in Canaan, so Jacob sent his 10 older sons to buy corn from Egypt. When Joseph's brothers appeared before him, they had no idea who he

ABOVE: *Joseph Explaining Pharoah's Dreams* by Jean Adrien Guignet (1816–54). Joseph is brought before Pharoah, at the butler's recommendation, to interpret the ruler's dreams.

was. He, however, recognized them at once, but pretended not to have, and accused them of being spies. They told him that they were brothers, and that their youngest brother had remained in Canaan. Joseph said that, to test whether their story was true, he would keep one of them as a hostage and the others must return to Canaan and bring their young brother back with them.

Simeon was kept behind and the other brothers returned, laden with corn and money. At first, Jacob refused to let them go back to Egypt with Benjamin, but when at last they had eaten all the corn and could only get more by returning to Egypt, reluctantly, Jacob agreed. He sent them off with Benjamin and gifts to placate the governor. The brothers were received graciously by Joseph, who released Simeon and invited them all to dine with him, but he still did not reveal himself.

The next morning, Joseph ordered his servants to fill the men's sacks with food and money, and to put his own silver cup into Benjamin's sack. Then after the brothers had set off, Joseph sent his servants to chase after them and accuse them of stealing his cup. The brothers, of course, denied the theft, and agreed that if one of them had the cup he should become Joseph's slave. When the cup was found in Benjamin's sack, the brothers were beside themselves with grief.

30

LEFT: Joseph was put in charge of the storing and distribution of corn. This illustration from The Golden Haggadah shows him supervising the distribution of food to the Israelites who had come to Egypt when famine struck Canaan.

Joseph said that all of them except Benjamin could go home, but Judah told him that their old father would die if he lost his youngest son. He explained that Benjamin's brother was dead, and that the remaining son of Rachel was his father's favourite. When Judah offered to remain as a slave in place of Benjamin, Joseph at last broke down and told his brothers who he was. The brothers were terrified of the vengeance he could exact now he was in such a powerful position, but Joseph told them that God had blessed all he had done, and he had forgiven them.

Joseph sent his brothers back to their father, laden with presents, and Jacob was overjoyed to hear that his son was alive. Eventually they settled in Egypt, under Joseph's protection.

THE OLD TESTAMENT

PALESTINE	REST OF WORLD
2050 BC-1550 BC	**2050 BC-1550 BC**
*c*1800-1600 BC Abraham, Isaac, Jacob and Joseph	2030-1640 BC EGYPT: Middle Kingdom, 11th-14th Dynasties
1640-1530 BC Hebrew groups settle in Egypt on borders of Canaan	1724-1686 BC MESOPOTAMIA: Reign of Hammurabi
	1640-1530 BC EGYPT: 2nd Intermediate Period, 15th-17th Dynasties
1550 BC-1000 BC	**1550 BC-1000 BC**
1550-1070 BC Canaanites under Egyptian control	1550-1070 BC EGYPT: New Kingdom, 18th-20th Dynasties
1250 BC Hebrew escape from Egypt (the exodus)	*c*1358-1349 BC EGYPT: Reign of Tutankhamun
1220-1200 BC Hebrew domination of Canaan begins under Joshua	1290-1224 BC EGYPT: Reign of Rameses II
1200-900 BC Philistines occupy the Palestinian coast	
*c*1200-1025 BC The Judges; Deborah; Gideon; Samson	
*c*1040 BC Samuel	
*c*1030-1010 BC Reign of Saul	
*c*1010-970 BC Reign of David	
1000 BC-800 BC	
*c*1000 BC Capture of Jerusalem	
c 970-931 BC Reign of Solomon; building of Temple in Jerusalem	
931-910 BC ISRAEL: Reign of Jeroboam I	
931-913 BC JUDAH: Reign of Rehoboam	
c 870-850 BC ISRAEL: Reign of Ahab; Elijah	
c 850 BC Elisha	
800 BC-700 BC	**800 BC-700 BC**
750 BC ISRAEL: Amos and Hosea	721-705 BC ASSYRIA: Reign of Sargon II
c 750 BC Isaiah	704-681 BC MESOPOTAMIA: Reign of Sennacherib

THE OLD TESTAMENT

PALESTINE	REST OF WORLD
732-724 BC ISRAEL: Reign of Hoshea	
721 BC Samaria falls to Assyrians	
700 BC-600 BC	**700 BC-600 BC**
627 BC Call of Jeremiah	626-539 BC MESOPOTAMIA: Neo-Babylonian Dynasty
604-587 BC Nebuchadnezzar conquers Palestine	606 BC ASSYRIA: End of the Assyrian Empire.
600 BC Habukkuk	605-562 BC MESOPOTAMIA: Reign of Nebuchadnezzar
600 BC-500 BC	**600 BC-500 BC**
587-538 BC Capture and destruction of Jerusalem, exile to Babylon; Daniel; Ezekiel	555-529 BC PERSIA: Reign of Cyrus II
538 BC The Edict of Cyrus, return from Babylon	539 BC MESOPOTAMIA: Cyrus II of Persia captures Babylon
537 BC Foundation of the Second Temple	522-486 BC PERSIA: Reign of Darius
520-516 BC Building of the Second Temple	
500 BC-400 BC	**500 BC-400 BC**
486 BC Malachi	486-465 BC PERSIA: Reign of Xerxes I
458 BC Ezra leads Jewish exiles out of Persia to Jerusalem.	465-423 BC PERSIA: Reign of Artaxerxes I; Jewish exiles return to Jerusalem
445 BC Nehemiah; rebuilding of Jerusalem	
	400 BC-300 BC
	336-323 BC GREECE: Reign of Alexander the Great
	331 BC EGYPT: Foundation of Alexandria
	331 BC PERSIA: Alexander ends the Persian Empire
	304-30 BC EGYPT: Rule of Ptolemies
300 BC-200 BC	
304-200 BC Judea is ruled by Ptolemies	

The Promised Land

ABOVE: *The Finding of Moses* by the Italian painter
Romanelli (1610–62). Pharaoh's daughter's maids
present her with the baby Moses, rescued from the
river. The cloaked figure is perhaps the baby's sister or
mother.

T HE STORY OF *the Israelites' delivery from Egypt, their wanderings in the wilderness, and their final settling in Canaan – the promised land – is told in the books of Exodus, Numbers, Deuteronomy and Joshua, while details of the religious law is in Leviticus. These books were written by various authors, probably at times ranging from the eighth to the second century* BC.

MOSES IN EGYPT
(Exod. 1–15)

The end of Genesis saw Joseph and his brothers settled in Egypt. From these first immigrants, an increasingly large population of Israelites grew over the generations. The Egyptians began to resent them, and treated them harshly, subjecting them to forced labour. When their numbers continued to increase, Pharaoh ordered all their newborn male babies to be killed.

MOSES AND PHARAOH'S DAUGHTER

A Hebrew woman bore a son, and hid him for three months, hoping to evade Pharaoh's murderous decree. When it became too difficult to hide him, she put him in a basket made of bulrushes, and laid it by the river. The baby's sister, Miriam, stood by to see what would happen.

Eventually Pharaoh's daughter and her maidens came down to the river to bathe. She discovered the basket with the baby inside and, realizing that this was one of the Hebrews' children, decided to save him. Miriam came forward and offered to find a nurse for the baby. She fetched her own mother, and the boy was given to her to nurse. When the child was weaned, his mother brought him to the princess, who called him Moses, and brought him up as her son.

MOSES' CALL FROM GOD

When Moses grew up, he became indignant about the way his people were being treated by the Egyptians, and one day he killed an Egyptian who was ill-treating an Israelite. His crime was discovered and he was forced to flee to Midian. He became a shepherd there, working for Jethro, the priest of Midian, whose daughter he married.

One day, Moses was tending the sheep when he saw a bush that looked as though it were on fire, but the bush was not burned. God spoke to Moses

from the flames, telling him that the Hebrews were to be delivered from Egypt and brought to Canaan, 'a land flowing with milk and honey'. He told Moses that he had been chosen to lead his people and must go to Pharaoh and ask him to release the Hebrews from Egypt.

Moses could not believe that God had chosen him, but God convinced him with a display of miracles, including turning his staff into a snake. When Moses protested his lack of eloquence, God said that he would use his brother Aaron as his spokesman.

ABOVE: While Moses was tending the sheep of his father-in-law, Jethro, God spoke to him from a burning bush. The hand-tinted illustration is from the John Brown Bible.

THE PLAGUES

Moses and Aaron gathered the Hebrews together and told them of God's promises. When they first approached Pharaoh, his reaction was to increase the workload and suffering of the Israelites. God encouraged them to approach Pharaoh again, but he refused to grant their request. Then God commanded Aaron to hold his staff over the waters of Egypt, and the water was turned into blood.

The gold mask of Tutankhamun, one of the many treasures from the tomb of the young pharaoh, which was discovered in 1922 by the English archaeologist Howard Carter. Tutankhamun reigned between 1361–1352 BC. As he died within a hundred years of Moses' lifetime, the discoveries from his tomb give us a good idea of what life was like for Moses as he grew up in an Egyptian palace. The tent-shrines and wooden chests which were found in the tomb are also of biblical relevance, for it is likely that the Tabernacle and Ark of the Covenant were constructed on similar lines.

Each time Moses and Aaron asked Pharaoh to let their people go, he refused, and at each refusal God brought down a plague upon Egypt. After the rivers of blood there followed plagues of frogs, lice, flies, boils, hailstorms and locusts. Eventually God said that he would kill all the firstborn of Egypt, both people and animals.

THE PASSOVER

The final plague, the killing of the firstborn, was to affect only the Egyptians, not the Hebrews. God gave Moses instructions for the Hebrews to eat unleavened bread for a week, and finally to eat a ritual meal. They should also mark their doorposts with lamb's blood so that when God came to kill the firstborn he would see the blood and pass over the house without harming the occupants. This was the origin of the Passover, which is still observed by Jews today.

THE CROSSING OF THE RED SEA

Moses and Aaron led the Israelites out of Egypt, but they were pursued by Pharaoh's horsemen and chariots. As they approached the Red Sea, God told Moses to hold his hand over the water. As he did so, a strong wind blew over the water, parting the sea, and allowing the Israelites to cross safely over dry land. When the Egyptians started to follow, Moses held out his hand again. The waters returned, overturning the chariots and drowning all the Egyptians and their horses.

THE WANDERINGS IN THE WILDERNESS
(Exod. 15–40; Num.; Lev.; and Deut.)

The Israelites spent 40 years wandering, mainly in the wilderness of Sinai, until they came to the borders of the promised land. The journey should not have taken this long, but their route became less direct as their fortunes changed. The people often complained about their sufferings, and even wished they were back in Egypt, but God, through Moses, met their needs, often miraculously.

WATER MANNA AND QUAILS

Three days after the crossing of the Red Sea, the Israelites came to a place called Marah where the

RIGHT: When Pharaoh refused to release the Israelites, Egypt was struck by a series of plagues. The engraving shows the plague of locusts which infested the houses and destroyed all the crops and vegetation in Egypt (Exod. 10:1–19).

RIGHT: This engraving shows the plague of frogs (Exod. 8: 1–14).

LEFT: The crossing of the Red Sea by the Israelites, while the pursuing Egyptians drown, is represented in this Italian fresco, painted by Bartolo di Fredi (c 1330–1410).

water was too bitter for them to drink. They complained to Moses, who cast a piece of wood into the water, which then became fit to drink.

When they reached the Sinai desert, there was no food for them, and again the people complained to Moses. Moses spoke to God, who promised to supply food. He would send food for them every morning, and they were to collect enough for each day, but on the sixth day they could collect a double portion, for the seventh day was to be a day of rest. The miraculous food was known as manna, and this was the staple diet of the Israelites for 40 years. If they disobeyed God's commands and gathered more than they needed, the manna would be rotten the next day. At one point, the Hebrews became tired of manna and craved meat, bitterly complaining to Moses about this. God's reaction was to send them meat – a huge number of quails – but as soon as they had gratified their craving, the people became ill and many died.

Once, when they were without water, Moses, obeying God's instructions, struck a rock with his staff, and water poured out of it.

MOSES ON MOUNT SINAI
The people moved on and set up camp at the foot of Mount Sinai, while Moses went up to the top of the mountain to seek the will of God. God told

ABOVE: Moses is seen here on Mount Sinai receiving the stone tables of the Law from God, while the Israelites apparently cavort outside their tents below. The engraving is by Giovanni Lanfranco (1582–1647).

RIGHT: One of Moses' many miracles during the 40 years wandering in the wilderness was when he struck a rock in the desert and water sprang from it (Exod. 17: 1–6). This portrayal of the event comes from an early Christian sarcophagus.

him that he would appear in a cloud, on the top of the mountain, and speak to the people. However, the people were frightened of being so close to God and sent Moses as their messenger to hear what God had to tell them.

Moses listened to God's words and then went to convey them to the people. Then God called him to the top of the mountain where he gave him two stone tablets, containing all the laws and commandments. Moses stayed on the mountain receiving God's instructions for 40 days and 40 nights.

The most important laws that Moses was given on the mountain were those that have come to be called the Ten Commandments (Exod. 20). However, God also gave Moses laws which touched on every aspect of life: morals, crime, commerce and, of course, religious life. Instructions were given as to the priesthood; the construction of the Ark of the Covenant and the Tabernacle; laws about the Sabbath; how rituals, feasts and fasts were to be conducted; and which foods were permitted and which forbidden.

THE GOLDEN CALF

The people became impatient waiting for Moses to come down from the mountain, so they went to Aaron and said that as their leader was missing,

he must make them a god to lead them. Aaron told them to bring him all the gold earrings that they owned. He melted down the gold and made a calf, and built an altar in front of it. The people worshipped the calf, declaring that it was the god that had brought them out of Egypt, and Aaron said the next day would be a feast day, devoted to the Lord.

The next day the people killed animals, some as sacrifices to their new god, and some for the feast, which degenerated into an orgy. God saw what they were doing and told Moses, threatening to destroy them. But Moses pleaded with God and he relented. However, when Moses came down from the mountain and saw the people feasting and dancing, he threw down the stone tablets he was carrying and grabbed the golden calf. He threw it into the fire to melt it down, then ground it into powder and mixed it with water. He then forced the people to drink this mixture, and also ordered the priests to have 3,000 of the people killed. Later, a second set of tablets was engraved, and the covenant renewed, in reconciliation.

SPIES SENT TO CANAAN

The Israelites left Sinai and continued their travels, until they came to the borders of Canaan. Then, because the people were fearful of what lay ahead,

Moses chose a representative from each of the 12 tribes of Israel to be sent into the promised land as spies. They were to find out whether the land was fertile, what fruit grew there, and how well fortified the towns were.

When the spies came back they reported that the land was fertile; they had brought back some grapes, pomegranates and figs to prove it. However, they said that the towns were very well fortified and the inhabitants were giants who did all they could to discourage the people from going in and taking the land.

Only two of the spies, Joshua and Caleb, tried to rally the people into having the courage to attempt to conquer the land. Their efforts were in vain, for the people were frightened and preferred to listen to the pessimistic majority.

God was angry with the 10 spies and with the people and he told Moses and Aaron that none of them over the age of 20 would enter the promised land except for Joshua and Caleb. Later, Moses and Aaron were themselves barred from entering the promised land, as God's punishment for their doubting him on another occasion where he caused water to spring miraculously from a rock to satisfy the Israelites' thirst.

AARON'S ROD

God told Moses to take sticks, or rods, from the leaders of each tribe, and to write the leader's name on each. The stick from the tribe of Levi was to have Aaron's name on it. They were to be placed in front of the Tabernacle, where God would reveal which man he had chosen as his high priest. The sticks were left overnight, and in the morning Moses saw that the rod with Aaron's name on it had produced buds, blossoms and almonds.

BALAAM AND HIS DONKEY

The Israelites began to make inroads into the border territory, capturing some of the Canaanite and Amorite towns. The king of Moab, Balak, became alarmed at their activities, and sent messengers to the prophet Balaam, who was then at Pethor, near the Euphrates River. He was ordered to come and put a curse upon the people of Israel, so that the Moabites could defeat them. But God appeared to Balaam, telling him that the Israelites had his blessing, and must not be cursed. So Balaam refused to go with the messengers.

Balak sent more messengers, with promises of rich rewards if Balaam agreed to curse the Israelites. This time God allowed Balaam to go, but as he

OPPOSITE: This engraving by Albrecht Altdorfer (c 1480–1538) shows Joshua and Caleb returning from Canaan with the fruit they had gathered at Eshcol (Num. 13).

BELOW: The story of Balaam's ass (Num. 22: 22–35) is represented charmingly, if somewhat anachronistically, by the Dutch painter Hans Bols (1534–93).

43

The River Jordan at Galilee. The Jordan flows from Mount Hermon, through the Sea of Galilee, to the Dead Sea. The valley has been inhabited from about 5000 BC, but the most settled areas have always been those around Galilee. The River Jordan features in both the Old and New Testaments. The Jordan Valley was chosen by Lot when he and Abraham divided their territories (Gen. 13). Joshua miraculously led the people through the river (Josh. 3). Elijah was taken up to heaven on the banks of the Jordan (2 Kgs 2: 1–15) and his successor Elisha healed Namaan of leprosy by telling him to bathe in the river (2 Kgs 5). Jesus was also baptized by John the Baptist in the River Jordan (Luke 3: 1–22).

rode along on his donkey, the angel of the Lord barred their way. The donkey turned off the road, but Balaam beat it until it returned to the path. Twice more the angel appeared to bar Balaam's way, and each time the donkey tried to avoid it, and was beaten. The third time, the donkey lay down, and Balaam started to beat it. Then the donkey spoke, remonstrating with Balaam for beating it.

Now Balaam saw the angel for the first time. The angel told Balaam to go ahead, but to speak only what the Lord gave him to say. Balaam arrived at Moab and presented himself to Balak, but three times he blessed the Israelites instead of cursing them, and then prophesied the destruction of Moab.

THE CONQUEST AND SETTLEMENT OF CANAAN
(Deut. 34; Josh.)

The Israelites continued to be successful in their military affairs under Moses. God gave Moses instructions for crossing the River Jordan into Jericho and entering Canaan, but told him again that he was not to lead the people into the promised land. Instead, Joshua was appointed as his successor, and on Moses' death the people recognized Joshua as their leader, and God promised to be with him in his conquest of the land.

RAHAB AND THE SPIES
Joshua sent two spies to go and explore Canaan, and the city of Jericho in particular. They went to spend the night at the house of Rahab, a prostitute of Jericho.

The king of the city had heard that there were Israelite spies in Rahab's house and he sent messengers to order her to surrender them. Rahab had hidden the spies on her roof, but she told the king's men that the strangers had left her house at sunset. The messengers went off to pursue the Israelite spies, but meanwhile Rahab went up to the roof and talked to them. She declared her admiration for the Israelites and their God, and she made them promise that when they destroyed Jericho they would save her and her family. Then she let them down from a window by means of a rope, giving them advice as to how to avoid encountering the king's men.

45

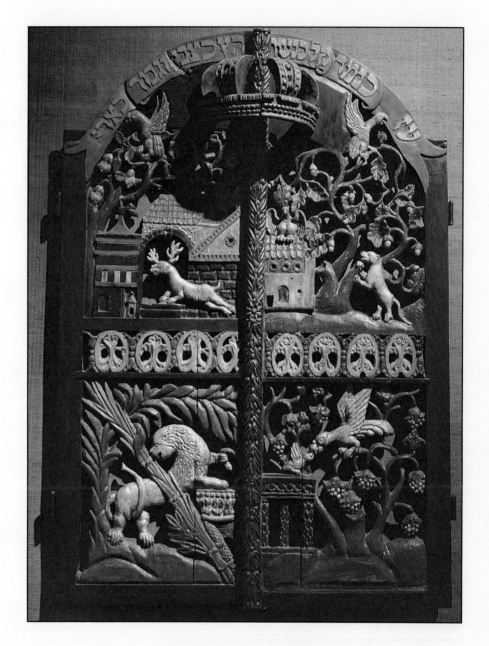

The Ark of the Covenant, an elaborately made box, was the most sacred object of the early Israelites. It was carried with them throughout their wanderings as a sort of portable shrine, held to be the actual home of Yahweh. It was given a permanent home when David brought it to Jerusalem and later his son Solomon established it in the temple, where it was housed in the innermost sanctuary. In later Jewish practice the ark became the place in the synagogue where the Torah scrolls (scrolls of the Law) were kept. The ark doors shown here are late seventeenth century and come from Krakow in Poland.

ABOVE: *The Israelites Crossing the River Jordan* by Badalocchio (1581–1647). The priests, directed by Joshua, are carrying the Ark of the Covenant through the miraculously dry bed of the River Jordan.

THE CROSSING OF THE JORDAN

The spies returned with an encouraging report and the people prepared to cross the Jordan. The priests went ahead with the Ark of the Covenant and, though the river was in flood, as soon as the priests put their feet in the water the river stopped flowing; the waters piled up far upstream, leaving the river near Jericho dry, and the people crossed with no difficulty.

THE FALL OF JERICHO

Jericho was a heavily fortified walled city, surrounded by locked gates, but God gave Joshua precise instructions as to how to capture it. For six days the people marched silently round the city, preceded by the priests, who carried the ark of the covenant and blew trumpets.

On the seventh day they marched around the city seven times. On the seventh circuit, just before the priests were about to blow their trumpets, Joshua told the people to shout. The priests blew their trumpets, all the people gave a great shout, and the walls of the city collapsed. The Israelites went in and killed all the inhabitants of Jericho, but Rahab and her family were spared.

THE SETTLEMENT OF CANAAN

After the defeat of Jericho, Joshua went on to lead his army to victory over the inhabitants of all the territory God had promised to the Hebrew people. At last they settled down in Canaan and Joshua assigned territory to each of the 12 tribes, and before he died he made the people pledge their loyalty and obedience to God.

THE ENEMIES OF THE ISRAELITES

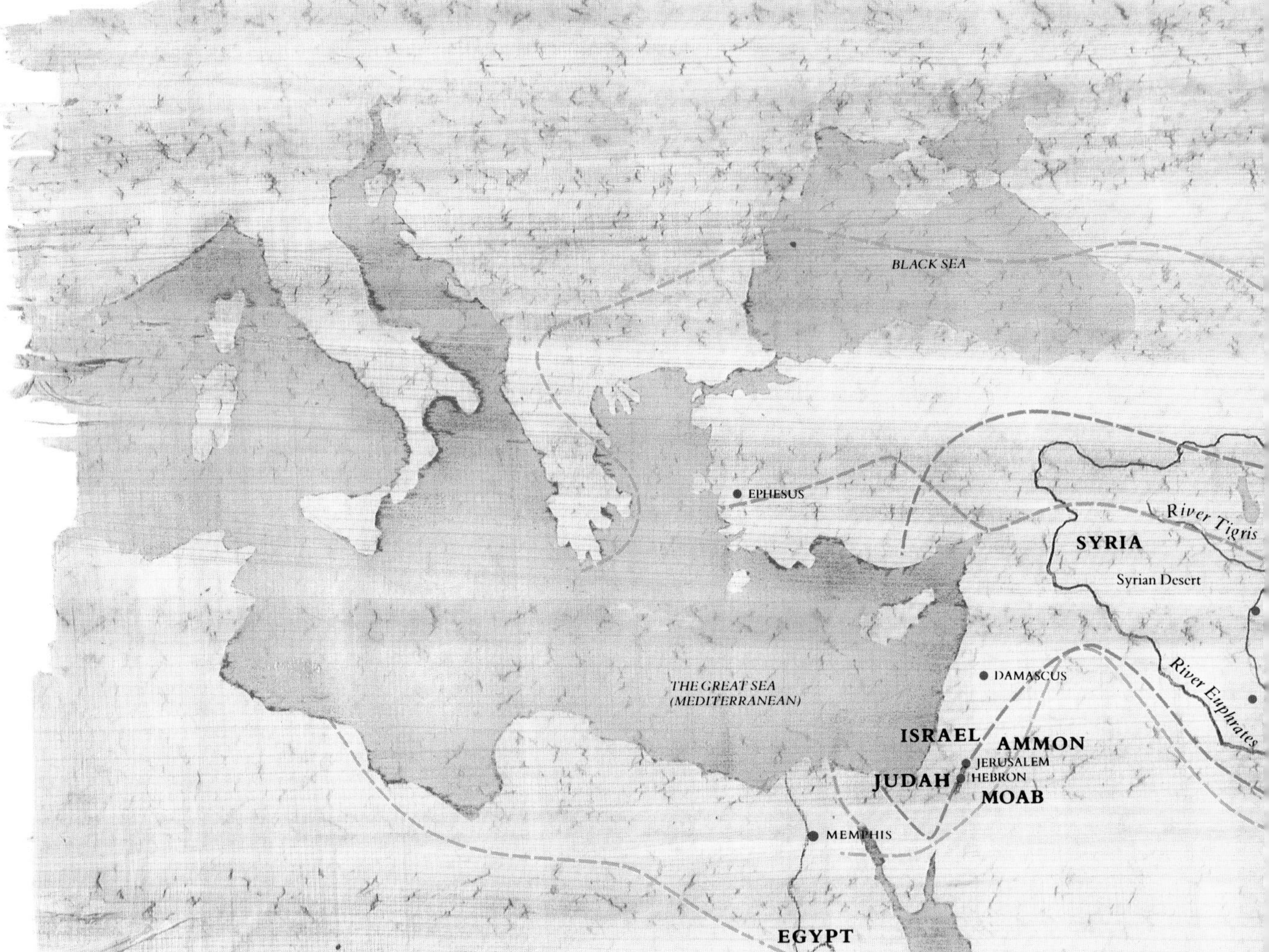

BLACK SEA

● EPHESUS

SYRIA

River Tigris

Syrian Desert

● DAMASCUS

River Euphrates

*THE GREAT SEA
(MEDITERRANEAN)*

ISRAEL **AMMON**

● JERUSALEM
● HEBRON

JUDAH **MOAB**

● MEMPHIS

EGYPT

● THEBES

RED SEA

Arabian Desert

River Nile

THE EXODUS

CANAAN ● JERICHO

DEAD SEA

● TANIS?

MOAB

● SUCCOTH

● ELATH

SINAI

MIDIAN

▲ Mount Sinai

EGYPT

River Nile

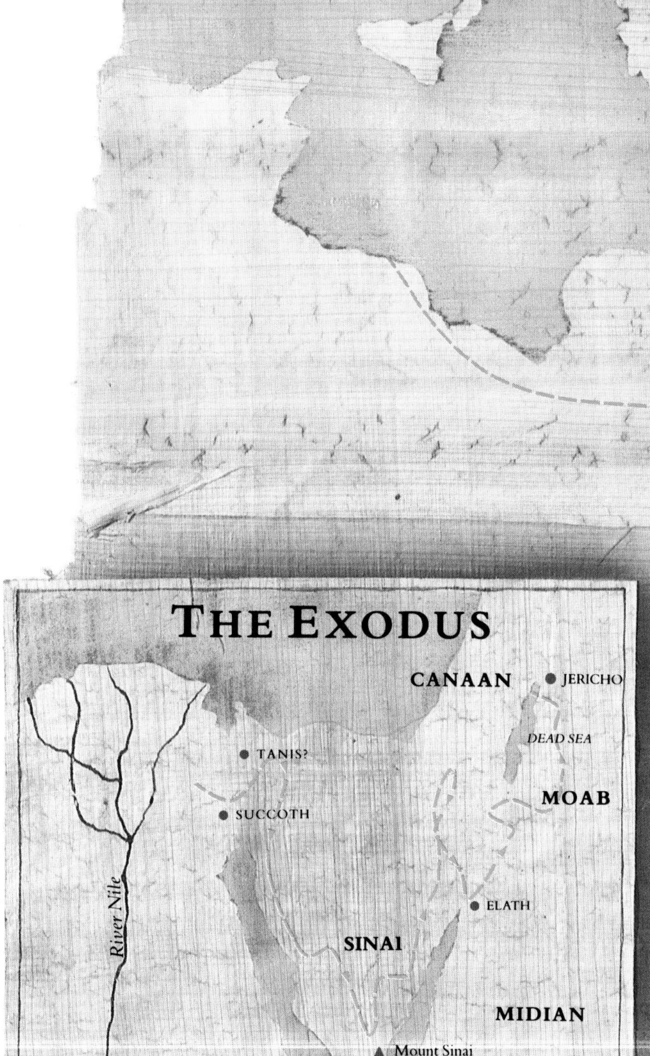

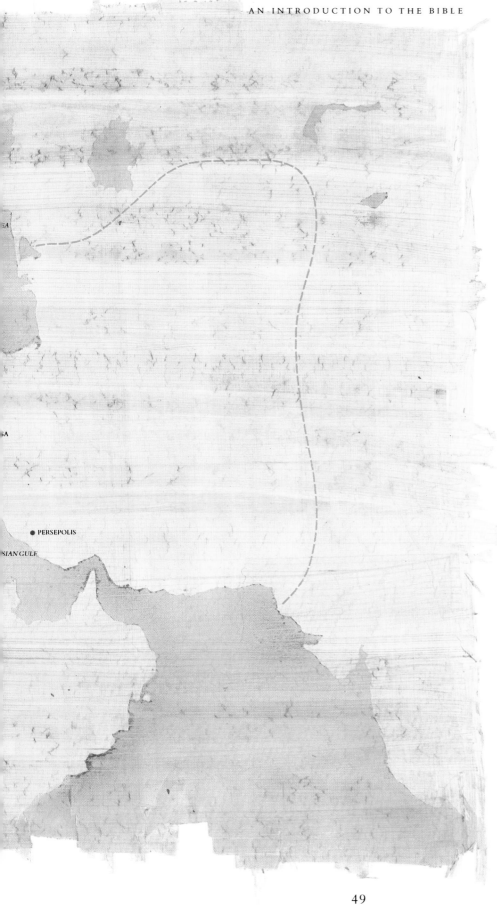

KEY:

● TOWN/CITY

▲ MOUNTAIN

— THE EXODUS
c 1250–1210 BC

— EXTENT OF
ASSYRIAN EMPIRE
LATE 8TH CENTURY BC

— EXTENT OF
BABYLONIAN EMPIRE
c 6TH CENTURY BC

— EXTENT OF
PERSIAN EMPIRE
c 500 BC

● PERSEPOLIS

SIAN GULF

The Judges and the Monarchy

ABOVE: An illustration from an 1816 edition of the
John Brown Bible shows Jael in her tent, in the act of
driving a tent-peg through the head of her 'guest', the
Canaanite captain, Sisera.

T HE PERIOD BETWEEN *the invasion of Canaan and the establishment of the monarchy is described in the book of Judges, and the book of Ruth is set in the same period. Both these books were once attributed to the prophet Samuel, but are of a much later date.*

The two books of Samuel cover the period of the monarchy to the end of David's reign, and the story is continued in the two books of Kings. These books were drawn from various sources, and probably edited into their final form by the fifth century BC. *The slightly earlier books of Chronicles give parallel accounts of the events related in Samuel and Kings.*

THE TIME OF THE JUDGES
(Judg.; Ruth)

After Joshua died, the people began to fall away from God. They intermarried with other peoples and worshipped idols. They were under constant attack from enemies, but God raised up leaders, known as judges, to rule over them.

ABOVE: Another hand-tinted picture from the John Brown Bible, which was first printed in 1778, illustrates the story of Jephthah, whose rash vow forced him to sacrifice his own daughter (Judg. 11).

DEBORAH, BARAK AND JAEL

The people continued to sin, and were conquered by a Canaanite king called Jabin who, with his captain Sisera, oppressed the Israelites for 20 years. The judge at that time was Deborah, and she sent for a man, a military leader called Barak, telling him to muster all the Israelite troops and go and fight Sisera's army at the River Kishon. Barak said that he would only go if Deborah went with him and she agreed to go, though telling Barak that now not he, but a woman, would have the credit of defeating Sisera.

Barak and his men descended on Kishon, took Sisera's army by surprise, and routed them completely. All the Canaanite troops were killed, but Sisera fled. He came to the tent of Jael, a woman of the Kenite people. He asked for drink and shelter, and Jael took him in, gave him some milk, and a bed for the night. When he was asleep, Jael took one of the tent-pegs, and a hammer, and she drove the peg into Sisera's head. As Barak approached, pursuing Sisera, Jael came out of her tent to meet him. She took him into the tent and showed him the dead body of his enemy.

GIDEON

The people sinned again, and now the Midianites began to conquer and oppress them. At that time an angel appeared to a young man called Gideon, saying, 'The Lord is with thee, thou mighty man of valour'. He told Gideon that he had been chosen to save his people from the Midianites. Gideon could not believe this, for he was of lowly birth. However, the angel showed him that he was from God when he touched the bread and meat that Gideon had brought him with his staff, and it was immediately burnt up.

That night, on God's instructions, Gideon built an altar to God, and tore down his father's pagan altars. He then sent messengers to rally the Israelite tribes to his side. He was still unsure of his call though, and he decided to put God to the test. He placed a fleece on the ground, and told God that if, in the morning, there was dew on the fleece but not on the ground, he would take this as a sign that he was really being called by God. God performed this miracle, but then Gideon asked for a further sign, and asked God to perform the miracle in reverse. Sure enough, the next morning there was dew on the ground but the fleece was dry.

Gideon had mustered a huge army but God said that it was too big: if such a large army defeated the Midianites, they would think they had achieved it by themselves, and would not give God the credit. Gideon cut his army down to 10,000, but God made him reduce it to only 300, and this tiny army defeated the Midianites.

JEPHTHAH

Jephthah was a man from Gilead. He was a renowned soldier but he was the son of a prostitute, so his father's legitimate brothers had rejected him and forced him to leave home. However, when Israel was at war with the Ammonites, the people of Gilead tried to persuade Jephthah to return to lead them against the enemy.

Jephthah said that he would lead them only if they agreed that, if he defeated the Ammonites, he should be their ruler. They assented, and Jephthah prepared for battle. Before he crossed the river into Ammon, Jephthah made a vow. He said to God that if he gave him victory, he would offer as a sacrifice the first person who came to meet him from his house on his return. Then he led his army out to meet the Ammonites.

The Ammonites were defeated by Jephthah's army, and he returned home. As he neared his

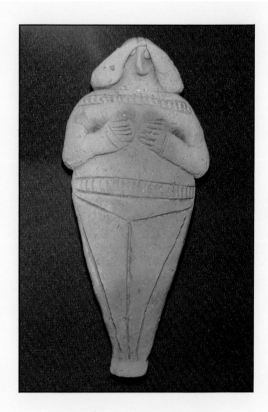

The first of the Ten Commandments forbids the worship of any gods but Jehovah. The Old Testament abounds with references to pagan deities and the struggles of God's prophets to prevent the people from joining in their worship. The principal goddess of the Mesopotamian region was Ishtar, goddess of love and war. The terracotta figure shown here comes from the ancient city of Ur and dates from about 2100 BC. Ishtar's Canaanite counterpart was Baal's consort Astarte, known to the Israelites as Ashtoreth.

house, his daughter, his only beloved child, came out to meet him, singing and playing on the tambourine. Jephthah was horrified, but both he and his daughter believed that it was not possible for him to renege on a vow made to God. The girl asked for two months grace, so she could spend time in the mountains with her friends mourning because she would die a virgin. Jephthah agreed, and after two months he sacrificed his daughter.

SAMSON

The Philistines conquered Israel and ruled over the people for 40 years. During this time, a barren Israelite woman was visited by an angel. She was told that she would have a son and he was never to cut his hair, for he would be dedicated to God,

ABOVE: *Samson and Delilah* by Rubens (1577–1640). While Samson sleeps in Delilah's lap, his hair is shorn.

and would deliver Israel from the Philistines. The baby was born and called Samson.

Samson grew up to be extraordinarily strong and became the judge over Israel. He was the sworn enemy of the Philistines, but could not resist their women. His marriage to a Philistine woman caused great distress to his family and quarrels with his in-laws which resulted in Samson killing 1,000 Philistines.

Later, Samson fell in love with a woman called Delilah, but she was in league with the Philistine rulers who promised her money if she could discover how Samson could be overpowered. She kept asking Samson the secret of his strength and he kept giving her false answers. Eventually she nagged and wheedled until he told her the truth: if his hair was cut he would become as weak as anyone else. While Samson slept, Delilah called the Philistines. They cut off his hair, then put out his eyes, chained him up and put him in prison.

The Philistine rulers met together to celebrate Samson's downfall, and called for him to be taken

out of prison and brought in to entertain them. Samson's hair had grown again while he was in prison and he had regained his strength. He prayed to God to give him revenge over his enemies, then he pushed against the pillars and the building collapsed, killing Samson and 3,000 Philistines.

RUTH

An Israelite family went to live in Moab during a time of famine, and the two sons married Moabite girls. When the father and both sons died, the widow Naomi was left with her daughters-in-law, Orpah and Ruth.

Naomi wanted to return to her own country, and she prepared to leave Orpah and Ruth. But Ruth loved Naomi and insisted on returning with her, saying, 'Whither thou goest, I will go. Thy people shall be my people and thy God my God.'

Ruth and Naomi settled in Bethlehem, where Naomi and her husband had come from. It was

ABOVE: The blinded Samson, in his final God-given show of strength, destroys the Philistine temple of Dagon, killing his enemies and himself. The engraving is by the Flemish artist Cornelius Matsys (1513–79).

harvest time and poor people then used to glean in the fields, picking up the bits of corn that the harvest workers had left behind. Ruth wanted to help to feed Naomi and herself so she went off to glean corn. The field where she went to work belonged to Boaz, a rich man who was a relation of Naomi's husband. When Boaz saw Ruth and found out who she was, he offered her protection and hospitality, and made sure she was able to gather plenty of corn.

It was the custom among the Israelites that when a man died without children his nearest relation would take on the responsibilities of redeeming his property and protecting his widow. At Naomi's suggestion, Ruth went to Boaz while he slept and lay at his feet, and when he woke she reminded Boaz of his responsibilities. After a nearer kinsman had rejected the opportunity, Boaz redeemed Naomi's property and married Ruth. Their son Obed became the grandfather of King David.

SAMUEL, SAUL AND DAVID
(1 Sam.)

The last of the judges was the prophet Samuel, and it was he who was responsible for ending this troubled time in the history of Israel and introducing a monarchy.

THE CHILDHOOD OF SAMUEL

Hannah was a barren woman who was grieved because of her childlessness. She vowed to God that if he gave her a son she would dedicate the boy to his service. God answered her prayer and she had a son, whom she named Samuel.

When Samuel was weaned, Hannah and her husband took him to the Lord's house and left him there with the priest, Eli. Samuel learned to serve the Lord under Eli, and saw his parents only once a year when they came to make a sacrifice to the Lord. Eli was of the tribe of Levi, and his priesthood was a hereditary office. He himself lived a blameless life, but his sons abused their priest-

ABOVE: In this painting by the English artist William Blake (1757–1828), Naomi is trying to persuade her two Moabite daughters-in-law, Ruth and Orpah, to return to their families, and not to follow her to Bethlehem.

hood and behaved scandalously. Although their behaviour grieved Eli, he barely reproached them for it.

One night Samuel was sleeping when he heard a voice calling his name. He ran to Eli, but the priest said he hadn't called him and told him to go back to bed. When Samuel heard the voice again, and then a third time, Eli realized that it must be God who was calling Samuel. He told the boy that if he heard the voice again, he was to say, 'Speak, Lord, for thy servant heareth'. God did call again, and when Samuel answered him, he told the boy that he would punish Eli's family because of the sons' wickedness, and their father's failure to prevent it.

After Samuel had grown up and became a recognized prophet, Eli's sons were killed in battle with the Philistines and the Ark of the Covenant was taken. Eli died when he was told the news.

SAUL IS MADE KING

Samuel became judge over Israel and ruled wisely but, when he began to age, and it was clear that his sons were not going to be worthy successors

Amalekites and others in battle. He personally led his troops, together with his son, Jonathan, who was also a fearless soldier.

THE ANOINTING OF DAVID

Saul began to disobey God's instructions, and God told Samuel that he had rejected Saul as king, and had chosen as his successor one of the sons of a man called Jesse, who lived in Bethlehem.

Samuel found Jesse, who brought out his sons to meet the prophet, but each time God told him that this was not the one, so he asked Jesse if he had any other sons. Jesse sent for David, the youngest, who had been out tending the sheep. Samuel immediately knew that this was God's chosen one, and he anointed David.

The spirit of God now fell on David, and at the same time it deserted Saul, who began to be troubled by fits of melancholy. His servants advised him to find a good harpist to play to him, and David was suggested. David was sent for, and remained in Saul's service, calming him with music whenever he was depressed.

DAVID AND GOLIATH

At that time Israel was at war with the Philistines, who sent out a man called Goliath of Gath to challenge the Israelites to produce a champion to fight him in single combat. Goliath was a gigantic man, around 10ft (3m) tall, and not surprisingly there were no volunteers. He issued his challenge every day for 40 days until at last David, who was actually only at the camp to deliver provisions to his older brothers, heard the challenge. He presented himself to Saul and volunteered to fight Goliath.

Saul offered David his own armour, but it was too heavy for him, and he took it off. He picked up five smooth stones and his shepherd's stick and catapult. When Goliath saw this unarmed boy coming towards him he mocked, but David took a stone and, carefully aiming his catapult, hit Goliath in the forehead, breaking his skull and killing him.

SAUL AND DAVID

After David had killed Goliath he went on to more military successes and was promoted by Saul, but eventually the king became violently jealous. All the people loved David, and even Saul's children seemed captivated by him. Jonathan and David had become devoted friends and Michal, Saul's

to him, the people came to Samuel and asked him to appoint a king. Samuel argued against this, but the people were adamant, and finally God told Samuel to give them what they wanted.

God told Samuel that he would send him a man from the tribe of Benjamin, who would be king and deliver Israel from the Philistines. The next day, a tall, handsome man called Saul approached Samuel. He was seeking out Samuel as a renowned holy man, for his father had lost some donkeys, and Saul needed wisdom as to where to search for them. Even before he told Samuel that he was from the tribe of Benjamin, God had told the prophet that this was the man. Samuel took Saul back to his house, and the next day anointed him.

After his anointing, God's spirit came upon Saul and the people readily acclaimed him as their king. Saul proved to be an effective military leader, defeating the Philistines, the Ammonites, the

ABOVE: An illustration of the much-loved story of the calling of Samuel. The child Samuel is shown with the priest Eli in this picture from the John Brown Bible.

OPPOSITE: *Triumphant David* by Elie Delaunay (1828–91). The young David stands over the body of Goliath. In one hand is the catapult with which he killed the giant; in the other the sword with which he cut off Goliath's head.

LEFT: 1 Samuel 25 tells the story of how Abigail averted David's anger when her rich husband refused him and his men hospitality, by coming to David laden with gifts of food and wine. *The Offering of Abigail* is by David Teniers the Elder (1582–1649).

younger daughter, fell in love with David. Saul decided to use Michal in a plot to bring about David's downfall. He offered his daughter to David as a bride but demanded in return a dowry of a 100 Philistine foreskins. The plot misfired; David killed twice the required number of Philistines and married Michal.

As David continued to flourish, Saul's jealousy grew, until he became determined to kill David. With the help of Jonathan and Michal, David managed to escape and he fled from Saul. He remained in hiding for many years, gathering a band of loyal followers around him, and continued to fight Israel's enemies. Saul still sought his death but, although David twice had the opportunity to kill Saul, he spared his life on both occasions.

ABIGAIL

David and his men came near to the town of Carmel, the home of a rich man called Nabal. David sent messengers to Nabal to ask him courteously for hospitality, but Nabal churlishly refused. David was ready to attack Nabal, but Nabal's wife, a beautiful and intelligent woman called Abigail, had heard of her husband's rudeness and its likely consequences. Without telling Nabal, she gathered together generous provisions and rode out to meet David. When she saw him she apologized for her husband and begged David to accept her gifts. Her charm and tact won David over, and he did not harm Nabal. When Abigail reported to her husband what had happened, Nabal had a stroke and died, upon which David proposed marriage to Abigail, who readily accepted.

THE REIGNS OF DAVID AND SOLOMON
(2 Sam.; 1 Kgs. 11)

During a battle with the Philistines, Jonathan and two other sons of Saul were killed. When Saul, who was himself badly wounded, heard of their deaths, he threw himself on his sword and died. David mourned for Saul and Jonathan and lamented their deaths. He then settled at Hebron where he was appointed king of Judah, and later king of Israel too. As a king he was notable both for his military victories and his worship of God. Early in his reign, he brought the ark of the covenant back to Jerusalem, but it was his son Solomon who was to build the temple to house it in.

OPPOSITE: An unusual illustration of the story of David and Bathsheba. In this detail from a seventeenth-century Norwegian tapestry the crowned figure is obviously King David, and Bathsheba is probably the figure near the bottom of the picture.

BATHSHEBA

David had many wives, beside Michal and Abigail, but it was his love for Bathsheba that caused him to lapse from his customary godliness. Bathsheba was a beautiful woman married to Uriah the Hittite, one of David's generals. When Uriah was away fighting, but David was at home, he saw Bathsheba bathing and was immediately attracted to her. He sent for her to come to him, and they made love.

Later, Bathsheba sent a message to David to say that she was pregnant. David sent for her husband to come back from the front, and encouraged him to go home to Bathsheba, hoping that Uriah would sleep with his wife and that the pregnancy would be attributed to him. When this ploy failed, David sent Uriah back to the front with a letter to Joab, David's nephew and military commander. David instructed Joab to put Uriah in the forefront of the battle, and then leave him defenceless. Joab obeyed, Uriah was killed, and David married Bathsheba.

Eventually the prophet Nathan opened David's eyes to the wickedness of his actions and he repented, but God punished him by causing the child that Bathsheba had borne him to die. However, Bathsheba conceived again, and gave birth to their son Solomon.

TAMAR AND ABSALOM

Absalom was David's third son, a handsome, charming young man who was his father's favourite and heir. One of his half-brothers, Amnon, fell in love with Absalom's sister Tamar. After tricking Tamar into visiting him, Amnon tried to seduce her and, when she resisted, raped her. His love now turned to contempt and disgust and he rejected Tamar and threw her out.

Absalom was absolutely furious with Amnon and plotted revenge: two years later he had Amnon killed, and he then fled. David forgave Absalom and they were reconciled but then Absalom began to gather followers around him and to organize a rebellion against his father. Eventually it came to battle between Absalom's faction and those who remained loyal to the king. David sent his men out to fight with Absalom's men, but begged them to spare Absalom himself. However, Absalom got caught by his long hair in an oak tree and was killed by Joab. On hearing of his death, David wept, crying, 'O my son Absalom, my son, my son Absalom! Would God I had died for thee, O Absalom, my son, my son!'

DAVID.

DAVID'S OLD AGE

At the end of David's reign he was very old and he was unable to keep himself warm, no matter how many blankets he put on. His officials found a beautiful young girl called Abishag to serve the king. She looked after him and lay close to him to keep him warm, but they did not have intercourse.

Now Absalom was dead, Adonijah was the eldest surviving son, and he expected to succeed his father. However, Bathsheba, backed up by the prophet Nathan, pleaded for her son Solomon to be the next king, and David promised that this would be done. After David's death, Adonijah asked to have Abishag as his wife, as a consolation prize for not becoming king. Solomon was infuriated by this request and had Adonijah killed.

SOLOMON'S REIGN

Near the beginning of his reign, Solomon had a dream in which God asked him what gift he wanted, and Solomon asked for the gift of wisdom. God was pleased with this request and promised him wisdom and great wealth as well. The wisdom of Solomon is illustrated by his famous judgement in the case where two prostitutes were in dispute over a baby. Both had recently given birth and one of the babies had died; now each claimed that the surviving child was hers. Solomon suggested that the child be cut in two and they could have half each. One woman agreed but the other said she would rather the baby was given to her rival than be killed. Solomon then knew this was the real mother and gave her the child.

Solomon became immensely rich and surrounded himself by luxury and expensive possessions. However, he used some of his wealth in his greatest achievement: the building of the temple to God in Jerusalem. Solomon also had an enormous harem and his many foreign wives eventually led him away from God and into idolatrous worship.

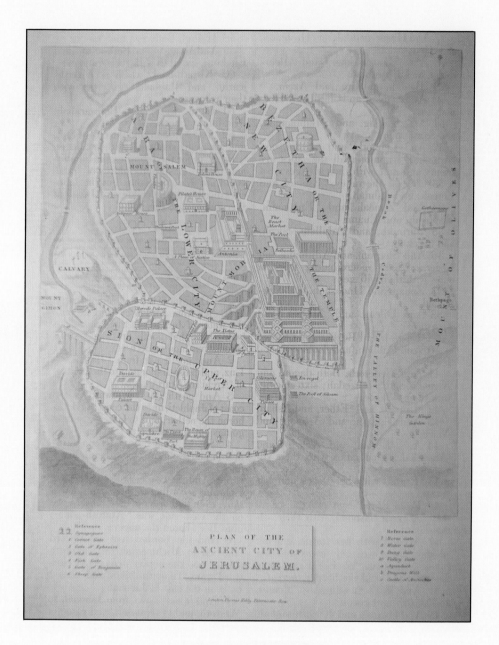

A plan of the ancient city of Jerusalem. The history of the city goes back to the Stone Age, and it had been settled by a variety of Semitic peoples before the Israelites entered Canaan. David captured the city and Solomon built the first temple there. The city was destroyed by the Babylonians in 587 BC and remained in ruins until about 445 BC, when Nehemiah ordered the rebuilding of the walls. The city was taken by Alexander the Great in 332 BC but was subsequently occupied by Egyptians and Syrians until temporarily recaptured by the Jews in 165 BC. Herod the Great rebuilt the temple in 37 BC, but it was destroyed again in AD 70.

64

THE DIVIDED KINGDOM
(1 Kgs. 12–22; 2 Kgs.)

God punished Solomon for his idolatry by taking away much of his kingdom and giving it to one of his officials, Jeroboam. From this time on the kingdom was divided into the larger northern kingdom of Israel, ruled by Jeroboam's descendants, and the smaller southern kingdom of Judah, ruled by Solomon's descendants. We have accounts of the reigns of many kings of Israel and Judah, good kings and bad, some faithful to God but many wicked and idolatrous.

AHAB, JEZEBEL AND JEHU

Ahab was the seventh king of Israel and a successful warrior but, under the influence of his wife, Jezebel, he persecuted God's prophets and encouraged the worship of Baal and Asherah.

BELOW: In 1 Kings 17: 1–6, the story is told of how the prophet Elijah, hiding from King Ahab, was fed on bread and meat brought to him by ravens every morning and evening. The engraving is by the Dutch artist Pieter Jansz Saenredam (1597–1665), after Abraham Bloemart (1564–1651).

Ahab was a man motivated by greed with a total disregard for justice, but it was Jezebel who was more actively wicked. Ahab became depressed because he coveted a vineyard belonging to a man called Naboth, who refused to sell it to him. Jezebel arranged to have Naboth falsely accused of blasphemy and stoned to death so that Ahab could take possession of the vineyard. The prophet Elijah denounced Ahab and prophesied a horrible death for Jezebel. This was fulfilled when Jehu was appointed by the prophet Elisha to succeed Ahab. Jehu set about wiping out every member of Ahab's family. He ordered Jezebel's servants to throw her out of the window.

ELIJAH AND ELISHA

Elijah was God's prophet during the reign of Ahab, and was notable both for his fearlessness in opposition to the king and for many miracles. Among these was the raising from the dead of a widow's son, and the relief of a drought in Israel which had lasted for three years. In this dramatic incident, Elijah challenged the prophets of Baal to meet him on Mount Carmel to see whose god could answer prayer with fire. The prophets of Baal killed a bull as a sacrifice but, however frenziedly they prayed, their god could not produce fire to consume their offering. Then Elijah built an altar and prepared a sacrifice. He soaked it in water and then prayed, and God sent fire to consume it. Elijah then killed all the prophets of Baal, and the same evening the rains came and ended the drought.

Elijah did not die but was taken up to heaven in a chariot of fire carried by a whirlwind. His ministry was inherited by the prophet Elisha who had served under him. Elisha's ministry lasted for 50 years under several kings, and was marked by many miracles.

THE END OF THE MONARCHY

The last king of Israel was Hoshea and during his reign, Samaria, the capital, was besieged by the Assyrians. They took the Israelites as captives to Assyria and settled in the cities of Samaria themselves. The Assyrians and later the Babylonians attempted to take Judah also, but for many years the kings of Judah managed to withstand them. However, in the reign of King Zedekiah, the Babylonian king Nebuchadnezzar attacked Jerusalem. The city fell, the temple was destroyed and the people of Judah were taken captive to Babylon.

NAAMAN CURED OF HIS LEPROSY

2 KINGS V 14.

LONDON THOMAS KELLY

LEFT: The captain of the Syrian army, Naaman, suffered from leprosy, but was healed when the prophet Elisha made him wash seven times in the River Jordan (2 Kgs. 5). The illustration comes from an 1816 edition of the John Brown Bible.

The Assyrian Empire was one of Israel's principal enemies for centuries and its culture infiltrated that of the Israelites. The Semitic god Baal was related to the Syrian thunder-god Hadad, and also to Bal or Bel, a warrior god and the principal deity of Mesopotamia. The illustration of Bal shown here is from a Phoenician relief. Phoenicia was a centre of Bal worship and the name survives in Carthaginian names like Hannibal.

BELOW: *Elijah's Sacrifice* by Albert Moore (1841–93) illustrates Elijah's triumph over the prophets of Baal.

THE POETRY AND WISDOM
OF THE OLD TESTAMENT

ABOVE: *Job Tempted by the Devil* by the Spanish artist Francisco Herrera (1576–1656). Satan's first assault on Job's faith was to afflict him with boils. The artist has included the potsherd with which Job scraped his sores (Job 2:8).

POETRY, USUALLY ACCOMPANIED by music, was an important part of the Israelites' life, both sacred and secular. There is much poetic language used in the Old Testament, but there are also complete books written wholly or partly in verse.

Another important Hebrew literary genre was Wisdom writing, in which the problems of life are tackled either in the form of advice or contemplation. Some of the Wisdom writings of the Old Testament are actually in the form of poetry.

JOB

The book of Job is an example of speculative Wisdom literature. It was traditionally thought to have been written by Moses, but there are very few clues either to authorship or date. Most biblical scholars place it around the fourth century BC.

Apart from the introductory and concluding passages, the book is written as poetry. It deals with the problem of unmerited suffering by telling the story of a blameless man called Job, who is subjected to bereavement, loss of wealth and great physical misery, in order to test his faith. The book includes long debates between Job and his friends about the nature of suffering and its relationship to sin. In the concluding chapters God answers Job, and at the end of the book his health and wealth are restored.

The book has enriched our culture with its image of Job as the epitome of patience in suffering, and the notion of Job's 'comforters' – counsellors whose advice and comments have the effect of depressing those in need of comfort – referring to Job's unhelpful friends. There is also some beautiful poetry in the book, notably Job's assertion 'For I know that my redeemer liveth, and that he shall stand at the latter day upon the earth: And though . . . worms destroy this body, yet in my flesh shall I see God' (Job 19:25–26).

ABOVE: *Israelites playing music before the Ark of the Covenant.* This engraving from the Lyon Bible of 1579 illustrates 1 Chronicles 16, which describes how David organized his musicians to play and sing before the Ark.

LEFT: Nearly half of the Psalms are thought to be the work of David. This portrayal of King David playing the harp is a detail from an eighteenth-century French organ case.

PSALMS

The Psalms are essentially poems which were intended to be set to music. The book appears to be a compilation of several collections of psalms, many written during the time of the monarchy, but some after the Babylonian exile. Nearly half are attributed to David.

The Psalms include songs of praise, thanksgiving, and atonement; pleas for God's protection; and expressions of hope in a Messiah. They were (and still are) used in synagogue services, and some are used for particular liturgical purposes, such as the 'songs of degrees' (or 'ascents') which were used as processional songs.

There is no rhyme used in this poetry but there is a characteristic rhythm, alliteration, figurative language, and use of acrostic devices. A common feature is the restating and amplification in the second line of a stanza of what was conveyed in the first, for example, 'I will sing

unto the Lord as long as I live: I will sing praise to my God while I have my being' (Ps. 104:33). This book contains some of the most beautiful poetry of the Bible; perhaps the best loved being Psalm 23, 'The Lord is my Shepherd'.

PROVERBS

The book of Proverbs is a fine example of the type of Wisdom writing that deals with advice and comment about life. Though traditionally thought to have been written in part by Solomon, the various parts of the book date from different times, but would not have been put together before the fifth century BC

The first nine chapters consist of reflections and exhortations on the nature of wisdom. The next twelve chapters present 'The proverbs of Solomon', and are mainly practical instruction on the life of wisdom and righteousness. Other 'sayings of the wise' reflect on religious and social responsibilities; these are followed by further proverbs attributed to Solomon, and the unknown Agur and Lemuel, ending with a poem in praise of virtuous wives.

The book is the source of some well-known quotations: 'Go to the ant, thou sluggard; consider her ways, and be wise' (Prov. 6:6); 'Pride goeth before destruction, and an haughty spirit before a fall' (Prov. 16:18); 'Train up a child in the way he should go: and even when he is old, he will not depart from it' (Prov. 22:6).

ABOVE: These etchings by Daniel Hopfer, who worked around the beginning of the sixteenth century, illustrates three of the Proverbs of Solomon (Prov. 10: 1–3).

ECCLESIASTES

Ecclesiastes is an example of speculative Wisdom writing, written in monologue form. Once thought to have been written by Solomon, the book is now ascribed to an unknown author writing around 200 BC.

The author calls himself 'the Preacher' and the book is a reflection on the meaning and purpose of life. He examines the nature of wisdom, pleasure, riches, and the inevitability of death. His conclusion is that 'all is vanity' and our only duty is to keep God's commandments. Much of the book consists of practical observations and advice, similar to that found in the book of Proverbs. Like that book, Ecclesiastes contains some memorable prose, notably the verses beginning 'To every thing there is a season, and a time to every purpose under the heaven' (Eccles. 3:1–8).

SONG OF SOLOMON

As its name suggests, this book was believed to have been written by Solomon, but it is now thought by many to have been written at a later date.

At face value the book is a collection of love poems, of a lyrical, personal, and often erotic nature. There is virtually no religious content, but the poems have often been interpreted as having allegorical significance as a portrait of God's love for his people, or of Christ's relation-

HOFFART GT VOR DEM VERDERBEN HER · VND STOLTZER MVOT VÑ DEM FAIL · SPRVCH SALOMO · XVI · C · M · D · XXXI ·

ship with the church. The poetry is perhaps most notable for its striking similes applied to the beloved, for example: 'Thy teeth are like a flock of sheep' (Song 4:2); 'Thy two breasts are like two young roes' (4:5); 'Thy navel is like a round goblet' (7:2).

LAMENTATIONS

The poems that make up the book of Lamentations were traditionally believed to have been written by the prophet Jeremiah, although they are now usually thought to be the work of more than one author. None are likely to date from later than the end of the sixth century BC.

The first four chapters are acrostic poems, written to a formal pattern, and the final chapter is similar in form to some of the Psalms. The content is a dirge-like lament for the fall of Jerusalem, comparing its past glories with its present desolation, and interpreting the fall as God's punishment for sin.

ABOVE: Another illustration from the book of Proverbs: 'Pride goeth before destruction, and an haughty spirit before a fall' (Prov. 16:18).

RIGHT: In the book of Lamentations, the fallen city of Jerusalem is likened to a weeping widow, bereft and betrayed. This illustration to the book comes from the John Brown Bible.

Exile

ABOVE: In Mesopotamia in ancient times, lions were often kept in captivity within the royal palaces, as in the story of Daniel (Dan. 6). This seventh-century BC relief of a lion hunt comes from an Assyrian palace.

HE FALL OF JERUSALEM and the carrying off of the Judeans into exile happened in 597 BC and is recounted in detail at the end of 2 Kings. The book of Daniel is partly an account of the experiences of some of the Jews in captivity in Babylon, but may not have been written until the middle of the second century BC. The book of Esther is concerned with Jews living within the Persian Empire during the same period, but was probably written in the later part of the second century BC.

The books of Ezra and Nehemiah, which deal with the return from exile after Babylonia had been conquered by the Persians, date from the third century BC.

DANIEL
(Dan. 1–6)

Daniel is regarded as one of the major prophets of the Old Testament. He was one of the Judaeans who were taken to Babylon after Nebuchadnezzar's forces conquered Jerusalem, but he was among a select group of young men chosen from among the exiles to serve at the king's court. They were selected for their noble birth, good looks and intelligence, and spent three years in training, learning the Babylonian language and customs. Daniel and his three friends Hananiah, Mishael and Azariah were given Babylonian names. Daniel was known as Belteshazzar and his friends became Shadrach, Meshach and Abednego.

Daniel and his friends were skilful at learning Babylonian literature and philosophy, but Daniel was determined not to forsake his religion. He refused to eat the food served to him which, though sumptuous, was unclean according to Jewish law, and insisted that he and his companions be given a vegetarian diet. Despite this resistance, the four of them impressed the king more than any of the other young men and became valued members of the court. When Daniel was able to interpret a dream of Nebuchadnezzar's that nobody else could explain he rose even higher in the king's favour and was given high office in the province of Babylon.

At Daniel's request his friends were also promoted and became high officials.

THE BURNING FURNACE
The king had a huge statue of himself made out of gold, and he called all the officials of the province to see the statue dedicated. Then it was declared that when they heard the music of trumpets and other instruments, everyone was to bow down and worship the statue. Anyone who refused would be thrown into a burning furnace. Shadrach, Meshach and Abednego refused to worship the statue and they were reported to Nebuchadnezzar. The

RIGHT: In this engraving by William Linton (1812–1897), King Nebuchadnezzar watches as Shadrach, Meshach, Abednego, and the godlike fourth figure, survive the fiery furnace unscathed (Dan. 3).

king was furious and sent for them. Although he threatened them with the burning furnace, the three young men absolutely refused to worship the statue. Nebuchadnezzar, in a great rage, ordered the furnace to be heated seven times hotter than usual, and for Shadrach, Meshach and Abednego to be thrown in. The king was amazed when he looked and saw not three but four men walking about in the furnace. They did not seem to be hurt and the fourth man had the appearance of a god. He called to the men to come out and Shadrach, Meshach and Abednego emerged, completely unhurt, without even a trace of burning on their clothes. Then Nebuchadnezzar praised their God, and promoted the three young men to even higher positions.

NEBUCHADNEZZAR'S MADNESS

Nebuchadnezzar had another dream which Daniel was called upon to interpret. This was a very embarrassing situation for Daniel for the dream meant that the powerful king would be punished for his pride and arrogance by seven years of madness, when he would be cast out from human society and would live like an animal. His sanity and kingship would be restored only when he became humble enough to admit that it was God and not he who had authority over the world. Daniel had the courage to tell this to Nebuchad-

nezzar and to advise him to stop sinning and oppressing the poor immediately if he wanted to avert this fate.

The king obviously failed to take Daniel's advice, for a year later he was boasting of his power and majesty when God struck him with madness. He was driven from human society and lived with the wild animals, eating grass, until after seven years he praised God and acknowledged his authority, and his sanity returned.

BELSHAZZAR'S FEAST

Nebuchadnezzar was succeeded as ruler of Babylon by Belshazzar. This king gave a great feast to which he invited 1,000 of his noblemen. He gave orders for the precious vessels which had been taken from the temple at Jerusalem to be brought in and used for their wine.

Belshazzar, his lords and his wives and concubines caroused, using the holy vessels to drink toasts to their gods. Suddenly a disembodied human hand appeared and began to write on the wall of the palace the words MENE, MENE, TEKEL, UPHARSIN. The king was terrified and offered rich rewards to anyone who could interpret what the mysterious writing meant. After all the court magicians and advisers had failed, it was suggested that Daniel should be sent for. Daniel boldly rebuked Belshazzar for his ungodly conduct and told him that the writing meant that the days

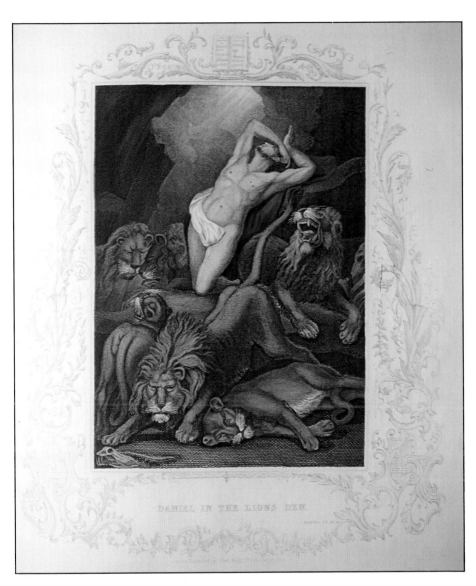

of his kingdom were numbered: God had weighed him in the balance and found him too light and his kingdom would be divided and fall to the Medes and Persians. That same night Belshazzar was killed and Darius the Mede took power.

THE LION'S DEN

Darius gave Daniel high office as an administrator and supervisor and was so impressed by his knowledge efficiency that he wanted to put him in charge of the whole empire. This caused jealousy and resentment among Daniel's colleagues, and they plotted how they could get him discredited, realizing that the best way to attack him would be through his religion.

Daniel's enemies persuaded the king to pass a law that said nobody could ask for anything except from the king, and anyone who did would be thrown into a den of lions. Then when they found Daniel praying to God these officials reported to Darius that Daniel was breaking his law. The king was unwilling to throw Daniel to the lions, but his law could not be changed, and he was forced to carry out the punishment. Daniel was put into the den, and in the morning the king came to see what had happened to him. He found that Daniel was completely unhurt. Daniel was taken from the den, and his accusers were thrown to the lions and killed. Darius made a new law commanding that everyone must respect Daniel's God.

LEFT: These illustrations to the first four chapters of the book of Daniel, featuring Daniel and Nebuchadnezzar, come from the twelfth-century Lambeth Bible.

THE PROPHETS OF THE OLD TESTAMENT

ABOVE: Isaiah is the greatest of the Old Testament prophets. This twelfth-century Romanesque portrayal of the prophet comes from the church of St Pierre in Moissac, France.

A PROPHET IS anyone who receives and utters revelation from God, and the Bible contains dozens of such people, from Abraham to John of the Apocalypse. However, there is a narrower sense in biblical terminology, where a Prophet is one of the writers of the Old Testament prophetic books. These are subdivided into the Major Prophets (Isaiah, Jeremiah, Ezekiel and Daniel) and the Minor Prophets (Hosea, Joel, Amos, Obadiah, Jonah, Micah, Nahum, Habakkuk, Zephaniah, Haggai, Zechariah and Malachi).

THE MAJOR PROPHETS

Isaiah was an eighth-century BC prophet. Although some of the prophecies in his book originate from Isaiah himself, the book is now widely believed to have three separate authors, the latest writing in the fifth century BC.

The first 39 chapters are the oldest and it is these that are most widely credited to the prophet Isaiah. These chapters contain political and spiritual prophecy, with the author foreseeing the eventual fall of Babylon and Assyria, but also speaking of the kingdom of peace and the coming of the Messiah. Chapters 40–55 are prophecies of freedom from the Babylonian exile and the restoration of Zion. The final chapters contain various prophecies, mainly of a spiritual nature. The book is valued greatly for its Messianic prophecies and the beauty of its language.

Jeremiah lived at the end of the seventh century BC. Much of his book originates from the prophet himself, though some portions may be the work of the scribe Baruch (who acted as secretary to Jeremiah), or of later scribes.

Jeremiah's ministry was spread over 40 years and five reigns, and he witnessed the fall of Jerusalem to Babylon. His personality – emotional, sensitive, melancholic – comes over more clearly than that of any other prophet,

ABOVE: This Italian woodcut shows the scene from the book of Ezekiel when God commands the prophet, in the valley of dry bones, to prophesy so that the bones will come to life.

LEFT: *The Vision of Daniel* by W Hamilton (1751–1801) shows the prophet with the angelic presence that he saw in a vision by the river Hiddekel (Dan. 10: 4–6).

by an unknown author long after the sixth-century events it decribes, possibly as late as the middle of the second century BC.

The well-known narrative section of the first six chapters is described elsewhere. The second half of the book is an account of Daniel's prophetic visions. These mystical prophecies have been the subject of many attempts at interpretation, particularly those relating them to the Antichrist and the Second Coming.

THE MINOR PROPHETS

Jonah was an eighth-century prophet, but his book is thought to have been written in the sixth century BC or possibly later. It is unusual among Biblical books of prophecy in being entirely in narrative form.

The story begins with Jonah being told by God to journey to the city of Nineveh, where he is to denounce the sinfulness of its people. Jonah rebels against God and takes a ship bound for the opposite direction. He is thrown overboard and swallowed by a large fish. The next chapter relates Jonah's prayer to God from the fish's belly. Jonah is delivered onto dry land and chapter 3 tells of how God again commands him to go to Nineveh. This time Jonah obeys and predicts the fall of the city. The people repent: a fast is proclaimed and even the king dons sackcloth and ashes. Because of their repentance God reprieves them from punishment. The final chapter describes Jonah's anger at

and his appeal is to the individual as much as to the nation. The message of the book is a condemnation of idolatry and immorality, lamentations for the sins of the people and a call to repentance, and prophecies of judgement and of the eventual redemption of Israel.

Ezekiel is believed to be the author of at least most of the book which bears his name, and dates from the end of the sixth century BC.

Ezekiel was one of those deported to Babylon and his message is to the Jews in captivity. Apart from the message of judgment and the need for repentance, the book is marked by its emphasis on ritual and its descriptions of the prophet's visions. These include the vision of the valley of dry bones which God brings to life (Ezek. 37:1–14).

Daniel is not now believed to have written the book of that name, which was probably written

Nineveh's escape from judgment. He shelters under a gourd which God then destroys, showing Jonah that, as he regrets the loss of the gourd, so God would pity the loss of so many human beings.

The other minor prophets lived mainly in the seventh and eight centuries BC, although Haggai and Zechariah were sixth-century, and Malachi fifth-century. The books were written from times varying from the fourth to the eighth century BC.

Many of these short books concentrate on calls to repentance and prophecies of doom, judgment, and destruction. Haggai and Zechariah deal with the restoration of the temple, and both contain Messianic prophecies, as does the book of Micah.

ABOVE: The large fish which is said to have swallowed Jonah has been identified with the whale, although older artists usually portrayed it as some unspecified sea monster. This engraving is by the Italian artist Agostino Carrachi (1557–1602).

The books of Amos and Micah are particularly striking in their social and political comment. Amos' message is notable for its stress on righteousness, both in a spiritual and social context. He denounces the empty religious ritual of his day, and in strong terms condemns the oppression of the poor by the wealthy. Micah condemns oppressive rulers and corrupt priests, but goes on to prophesy a time of peace and righteousness. This section contains the famous passage, which echoes Isaiah 2:4, '. . . and they shall beat their swords into plowshares, and their spears into pruninghooks: nation shall not lift up a sword unto nation, neither shall they learn war any more. But they shall sit every man under his vine and under his fig tree; and none shall make them afraid . . .' (Mic. 4:3–4).

ESTHER

The story of Esther centres on the Persian king Ahasuerus, who is thought to be the same person as Xerxes I, who ruled from 485–465 BC. The events take place in the winter palace at Susa (or Shushan) in southwest Persia, and are commemorated annually in the Jewish festival of Purim.

ESTHER BECOMES QUEEN

King Ahasuerus gave a huge banquet to which he invited every man in Susa. It lasted for a week and everyone could drink as much wine as he wanted. Meanwhile his queen, Vashti, was giving a banquet for the women. On the last day Ahasuerus decided he wanted to show off Vashti's beauty to all his guests, so he sent servants to fetch her. Vashti had no wish to be displayed in front of a crowd of drunken men and she refused to come. Ahasuerus was angry and asked his advisers what he should do. They declared that if the king let Vashti get away with this public display of rebellion it would upset the balance of power in every household in the country. If it was known that the queen had defied her husband then all the women in the empire would follow her example. On their advice, Ahasuerus banished Vashti and sent round a proclamation saying what he had done.

RIGHT: In this painting by Ernest Normand (1857–1923), Esther is denouncing the wicked Haman to the king.

Ahasuerus became restless and depressed and his advisers suggested that he send officials to hunt for all the beautiful young virgins in the empire and bring them to the palace. Then he could choose the one he liked best and make her queen. The king agreed to this plan.

There was a Jew called Mordecai living in Susa, who was one of the original captives taken from Judah. He had a beautiful young cousin named Esther, an orphan whom Mordecai had brought up as his own daughter. When Esther was chosen to be taken to the palace Mordecai warned her not to tell anyone that she was Jewish. The chosen girls spent a year being groomed and massaged before being presented to the king one by one. Eventually it was Esther's turn to appear before Ahasuerus. The king liked her better than any of the other girls and made her his queen.

HAMAN'S PLOT

Mordecai managed to obtain an administrative position in the palace, and was responsible for averting an assassination attempt on the king. Ahasuerus then appointed a man called Haman as his prime minister, and ordered all his officials to bow to him. Mordecai refused and, when Haman realized it was because Mordecai was Jewish, he became enraged not just with him but with the entire Jewish race. He spoke to the king about the rebellious nature of these people and gained his permission to order every single Jew in the empire to be killed.

When the proclamation declaring the forthcoming massacre was made public in Susa, Mordecai and all the other Jews there were in despair. Mordecai sent a message to Esther telling her to maintain her secrecy about her own origins, or she too would be killed. Esther replied, asking Mordecai to fast and pray for three days and she would do the same. After three days, Esther invited Ahasuerus and Haman to a banquet. Meanwhile, Haman had prepared gallows to hang Mordecai, but that night Ahasuerus discovered for the first time that Mordecai had once been responsible for preventing an assassination attempt on him, but had never been rewarded. When the king ordered that Mordecai was to be given royal robes, and be honoured publicly, it became impossible for Haman to have him hanged.

At Esther's banquet, Ahasuerus told the queen to ask him for anything she wanted and Esther told him that her people were about to be destroyed on Haman's orders. Ahasuerus ordered that Haman was to be hanged immediately on the gallows he had built for Mordecai.

Although Esther begged Ahasuerus to prevent the massacre, the proclamation which ordered it had the royal seal, and could not be stopped. However, Ahasuerus allowed Esther and Mordecai to send out letters with the royal seal to Jews in every province of the empire, warning them to defend themselves. So the Jews prepared and armed themselves, and on the day appointed for their destruction, they fought back and killed all their enemies.

At the time of the events in the books of Esther and Daniel, the Persian Empire dominated western Asia and spread into Egypt and Libya. Darius I (who ruled from 521–485 BC) established a winter palace at Susa, which is where Ahasuerus and Esther would have lived. The site of the palace and citadel was identified by archaeologists in the mid-nineteenth century, and many extraordinary discoveries were made there over the next fifty years, including the Code of Hammurabi. These enamelled bricks from the walls of the palace depict a griffon, a creature which was connected to sun worship and supposed to guard treasure.

THE RETURN FROM EXILE
(Ezra, Neh.)

When Cyrus ruled the Persian empire, he allowed a group of Jewish exiles to return to Jerusalem and start to rebuild the temple there. He also returned the cups and bowls that Nebuchadnezzar had stolen from the temple. The rebuilding of the temple started in about 536 BC, but it immediately encountered opposition from the people who had settled in Judah during the Jewish exile. This opposition continued throughout the reign of Cyrus and his successor Darius. However, Darius eventually realized that it had been Cyrus himself who had decreed that the temple be rebuilt, and he ordered the building to recommence. The temple was finished and dedicated in 516 BC.

Although the temple was rebuilt, the city of Jerusalem was still in ruins and any attempts to rebuild it met with fierce opposition. This situation lasted throughout the reigns of Darius and Xerxes, and at first King Artaxerxes also supported the opposition to the Jews' plans. But in 458 BC Artaxerxes allowed Ezra, a prominent Jewish scholar, to leave for Jerusalem taking with him all the Jewish people in the empire who wished to return to their homeland.

About 14 years after this, Nehemiah, who was a pious Jew and an official under Artaxerxes, learned that the Jews who had returned were still being oppressed and that the city walls and gates were still in ruins. He asked the king for permission to return to Jerusalem and start to rebuild the city walls. Artaxerxes gave him permission and sent him back with the official position of governor of Judah. Nehemiah encouraged the Jews to start rebuilding the walls, and he overcame the local opposition by arming the men who were engaged on the building.

Jerusalem was rebuilt but many of the returned Jews had fallen away from God, forgotten the law, and intermarried with gentiles. The people needed spiritual leadership and Ezra took on this task. He put a stop to mixed marriages and instituted proper observance of God's law and worship in the temple.

OPPOSITE: After the years of exile, the walls of Jerusalem were rebuilt under the supervision of the prophet Nehemiah. This illustration of the building comes from the John Brown Bible.

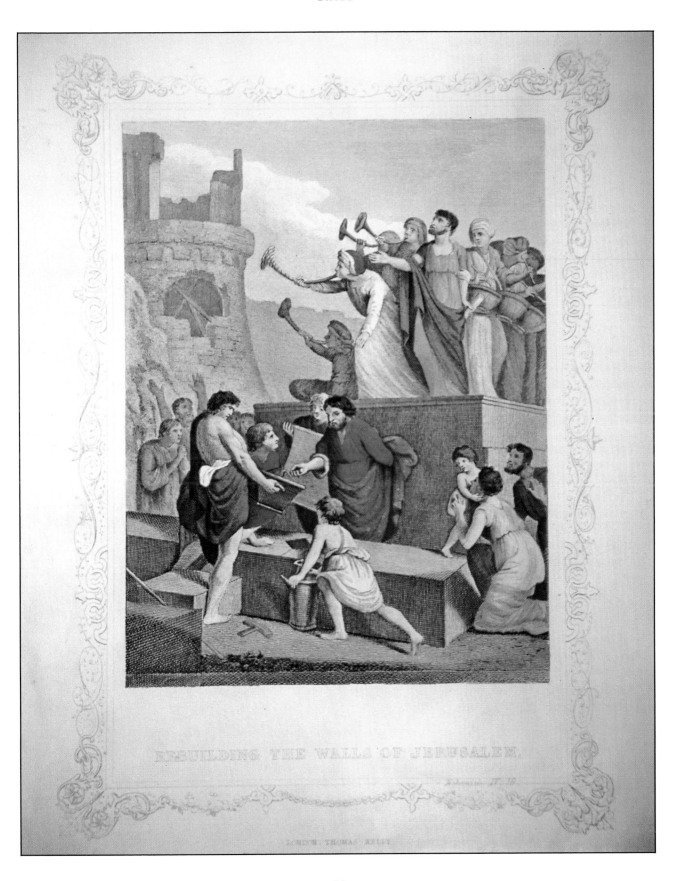

REBUILDING THE WALLS OF JERUSALEM.

LONDON: THOMAS KELLY

THE OLD TESTAMENT APOCRYPHA

THE WORD 'APOCRYPHA' comes from a Greek word meaning 'hidden'. It is applied to all the books of Scripture which are not included in the Protestant Bible, but particularly to the Old Testament books which are included in Roman Catholic versions. There are many other apocryphal books of both Old and New Testaments, which have been rejected as spurious or of doubtful authenticity, and these are now usually referred to as 'pseudepigrapha'. The apocryphal books include some of the most entertaining stories of the Bible, which have often been used as subjects by artists. These are described in some detail below, while the other apocryphal books are touched on briefly.

TOBIT

This story, sometimes known as 'Tobias', dates from the Babylonian exile. It tells of Tobit, a godly and faithful Jew in captivity in Nineveh. Tobit made it his business to bury the Hebrew dead, and he got into trouble for doing this and became impoverished and blind.

Tobit summoned his son Tobias and, after giving him general counsel and advice, instructed him to go to Media to collect a debt for him. Tobias was guided in his journey by the archangel Raphael in disguise. The first night they stopped by the River Tigris, where Tobias was attacked by a huge fish. With Raphael's help he killed the fish, which they ate, keeping the liver.

The angel told Tobias that they would lodge with a kinsman of Tobias's family, whose only child was a daughter, Sara. She had been given to seven men in marriage, but each one had been killed by the demon, Asmodeus, on their wedding night. Raphael told Tobias that Sara was his for the asking and instructed him how to avoid the fate of her previous bridegrooms. Sara and Tobias were married and, acting on Raphael's advice, Tobias burnt part of the liver

ABOVE: *Tobias and the Angel* by the French artist Jean-Charles Cazin (1841–1901).

OPPOSITE: Many artists have portrayed the dramatic story of Judith and Holofernes. This painting is the work of an Italian woman artist, Artemisia Gentileschi (1593–1652), who painted several pictures on the theme.

of the fish, and the smoke drove the demon away. After collecting the debt for his father, Tobias returned to his father, whose sight he restored, again using the liver of the fish.

JUDITH

The story dates from a second-century BC Hebrew source. It is set at the time when the Assyrian King Nebuchadezzar was attacking Israel. The king's general, Holofernes, asked Achior, the Ammonite captain, for information about the Israelites, and was given a brief his-

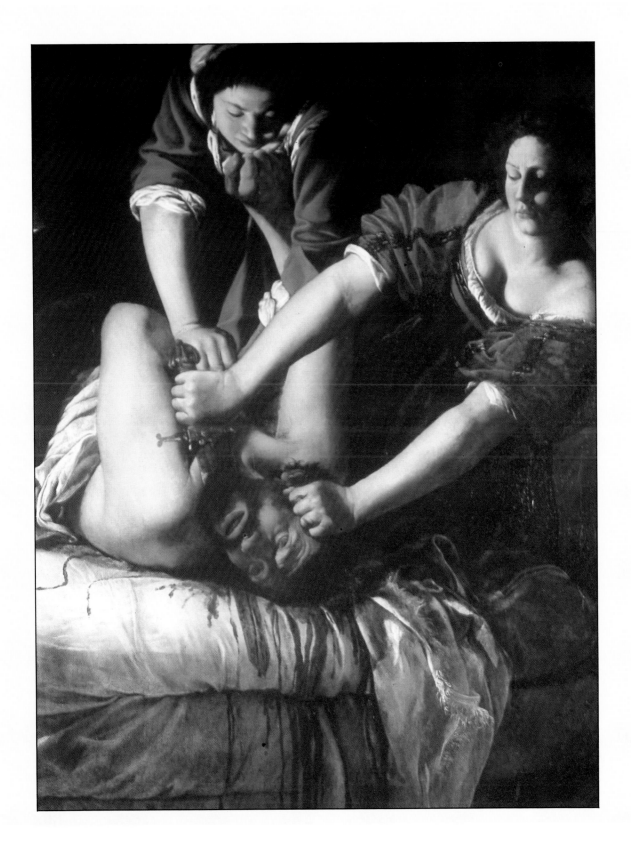

tory of the Hebrew people. Holofernes was furious at Achior's suggestion that these people were always protected by their God, and vowed to massacre them all, and then to torture Achior to death.

Achior was bound, but rescued by the Israelites of the city of Bethulia. He told them Holofernes' plans and, despairing, they planned to yield to the Assyrian army. But there was a woman called Judith living in Bethulia, a beautiful and godly widow, who begged them to do nothing until she had carried out her own plan to save them. Judith prayed and then adorned herself and, with her maidservant, made for Holofernes' camp.

Judith pretended to have military secrets to impart and was allowed into the camp and taken to Holofernes' tent. He was captivated by her beauty and asked her to dine with him. Judith encouraged him to drink freely and, when he

ABOVE: This picture of the virtuous Susanna, accused of adultery by the treacherous elders whose advances she had spurned, is by Antoine Coypel (1661–1722).

was in a drunken sleep, cut off his head. When she and her maid returned to the city and showed the people Holofernes' head, they were encouraged to pursue the enemy who, finding their captain dead, fled from them.

SUSANNA AND THE ELDERS

The story of Susanna is one of several additions to the book of Daniel, following from the end of the prophecies of Daniel. It tells of a beautiful and pious woman married to a rich Babylonian. Two elders of the people became inflamed with lust for her, and hid themselves in her husband's orchard so they could watch her bathing. They waited until she was alone and then appeared, asking Susanna to lie with them. When she rejected their advances, they had her falsely accused of adultery, claiming that they had surprised her with a young man in the orchard.

The people believed the elders and Susanna was condemned to death. But Daniel appeared and persuaded the people to let him cross-examine the elders to establish the truth. By interviewing the elders separately, and getting inconsistent stories, he proved that they were lying. The people accepted Susanna's innocence, and put the elders to death.

OTHER APOCRYPHAL BOOKS

I Esdras gives a parallel account of history recorded in the books of Chronicles, Ezra and Nehemia. There is also an addition, known as the 'Debate of the Three Youths', which is an adaptation from a Persian story.

2 Esdras is an account of seven visions and is also known as 'The Apocalypse of Ezra'. It derives from a Hebrew source but has been expanded with Christian additions.

Additions to Esther are regarded by most scholars as additions to the original Hebrew, though some maintain that the Hebrew canonical work is an abbreviated version. The extra passages include accounts of Mordecai's dream and an interpretation of it; the king's orders for the massacre of Jews and his subsequent edict permitting the Jews to defend themselves; prayers of Mordecai and Esther; and Esther's audience with the king.

The Wisdom of Solomon is an anonymous work, having its roots in traditional Jewish Wisdom writing, but almost certainly actually composed in Greek. The content is praise of wisdom and exhortation to seek after it.

Ecclesiasticus consists of the wisdom of sayings of Joshua ben Sira, who lived in Jerusalem around 180 BC. The translation was made by the author's grandson. It recommends observance of the law and a pious fear of God, and gives advice for daily living. The final chapters are devoted to the praise of the patriarchs and heroes of the Old Testament, and of Simon the high priest, who lived about 200 BC

Baruch is supposedly the work of the scribe or secretary of the prophet Jeremiah but is, however, thought to be of composite authorship. It contains an address by Baruch to the exiles in Babylon, prayers, praise of wisdom, and a lament for the captives, with a final assurance that they will be restored to their home.

Additions to Daniel are derived from the Septuagint. The first addition comes in chapter 3, and consists of the prayer of Azariah (Abednego) in the fiery furnace, in which he praises God's mercy and prays for deliverance, and the Song of the Three Holy Children, a song of praise uttered as they walked unharmed in the fire. After the story of 'Susanna and the Elders' in chapter 13, there follows the story of Bel and the Dragon, written to mock idolatrous worship. In it Daniel proves to the king that neither the idol Bel or a dragon, who was also an object of worship, are living gods.

The Prayer of Manasseh is thought to be Jewish in origin but is not known before the third century AD. In 2 Chronicles 33 the reign of Manasseh, son of Hezekiah, is described. He was a worshipper of Baal and other idols, and heavily involved in occult practices. He was captured by the Assyrians and in his affliction prayed to the God of his fathers for release. God heard him and Manasseh was released, subsequently restoring the worship of God to Judah. This book purports to be his prayer when in captivity.

1 and 2 Maccabees are concerned with Jewish history between 175 and 134 BC and the heroic family of the Maccabees, particularly Judas Maccabaeus. It describes their struggles against the Syrian King Antiochus Epiphanes, the Hasmonean wars, and the line of priest-kings that they established. The first book was translated from a Hebrew work, apparently in about 100 BC. The second book is said to be extracted from a work by Jason of Cyrene, who is otherwise unknown.

BELOW: The apocryphal story of Bel and the Dragon mocks the worship of the Babylonian god Bel (also known as Marduk), and the dragon which was the god's symbol. This representation of a dragon is a relief on glazed brick from the Ishtar gate at Babylon, dating from the reign of King Nebuchadnezzar (604–562 BC).

The Life of Jesus

ABOVE: The four evangelists – Matthew, Mark, Luke
and John – are shown in this hand-tinted illustration
from an 1816 edition of the John Brown Bible.

HE NEW TESTAMENT *starts with the three 'synoptic Gospels' (Matthew, Mark and Luke), which give a broad view of the life of Jesus, and there is considerable overlap in the content. Traditionally thought to have been written by the apostle Matthew, the first Gospel is now believed to be of unknown authorship and to date from about AD 85 to 90. Apparently written specifically for a Jewish audience, it contains many references to Old Testament prophecies about the Messiah, and there is an emphasis on Jesus's ethical teaching, which is presented as a fulfilment of the Jewish law.*

Mark's Gospel is thought to have been written by Mark of Jerusalem, the companion of Paul and Barnabas, between AD 65 and 70. The Gospel is a simple straightforward account of Jesus's life, and is the source for much of Matthew's and Luke's Gospels. The book appears to have been written for gentiles, for there is little reference to the Old Testament.

Luke's Gospel was almost certainly written by the physician and companion of Paul. It is of uncertain date, but it was probably written in the last quarter of the first century AD and uses both Matthew and Mark for source material. Luke gives us the fullest account of the birth and early life of Jesus and emphasizes the humanitarian aspects of Jesus's ministry: his concern for sinners and outcasts, the poor, the sick, and women.

The Gospel of John was traditionally believed to have been written by the apostle John, but is now thought to be of unknown authorship, although it may have been partly dictated by the apostle to an associate. It probably dates from between AD 90 and 110. John's Gospel differs from the other three in many ways. It is less an account of Jesus's life and ministry than an attempt to interpret these events spiritually, revealing Jesus as the Messiah and Son of God. There is much figurative language and Jesus's discourses are longer and more abstract than in the other Gospels.

BIRTH AND BOYHOOD
(Matt. 1–2; Luke 1–2)

Mary was a young virgin living in Nazareth in Galilee, and betrothed to a carpenter called Joseph. She was visited by the angel Gabriel who told her that she would become pregnant and bear a child by the Holy Ghost. Joseph, too, was visited by an

angel in a dream who told him not to hesitate to marry Mary, for the child she was expecting would be the saviour of the world.

Joseph and Mary travelled to Bethlehem in Judaea, for there was a census being taken, and that was where they had to register. The town was crowded and there was no room for them to stay in the inn, so they lodged in a stable, and it was there that the baby, Jesus, was born. That night a group of shepherds who were tending their flocks in the countryside nearby had a vision of angels who told them of the birth of a saviour in Bethlehem. They set off to the town and found Mary and Joseph, and the baby lying in a manger in the stable.

Joseph and Mary took the child to be presented to God in the temple at Jerusalem. There he was

ABOVE: Books of Hours were illustrated prayerbooks used by lay people for private devotions. The Hours of the Office of the Virgin were illustrated by appropriate pictures, and traditionally 'The Adoration of the Magi' went with the hour of Sext. The example shown here is from the fifteenth-century, French, Margaret de Foix Book of Hours.

Herod the Great was responsible for the erection of many magnificent buildings, and their ruins have been discovered at Jericho and Jerusalem. More recent archaeological work has unearthed important Herodian remains at Masada, west of the Dead Sea, the site of which is shown in this photograph. Israeli archaeologists in the 1960s found the remains of the fortress and two palaces that Herod built in these isolated rocks, and the reservoirs cut into the rock to supply water to the fortress. The fortress was later used by Jewish zealots holding out against the Roman occupation in AD 66–73, and the remains of a synagogue and ritual baths from this period, as well as leather scrolls with biblical texts, have been found.

recognized as the Messiah by two devout old people: Simeon, who had been promised by God that he would not die before he had seen the Messiah, and a prophetess named Anna.

KING HEROD

Herod the Great was king at the time that Jesus was born. Some wise men from the East told him that they had been following a star which they believed was a sign that the king of the Jews had been born, and the priests confirmed that it was prophesied that the Messiah would be born in Bethlehem. Herod told the wise men to go to Bethlehem and find the baby, pretending that he too wished to worship the child.

The wise men travelled to Bethlehem where they found the child Jesus, and they worshipped him and presented him with gifts of gold, frankincense and myrrh. They did not report back to Herod, having been warned against doing so in a dream, but returned to their country. Joseph, too, had a dream warning him of Herod's evil intentions, and so the family fled to Egypt.

When Herod realized that the wise men were not going to return he determined to destroy the child they had spoken of. He ordered the slaughter of every male child in Bethlehem under two years

ABOVE LEFT: Jesus was taken by Mary and Joseph to be presented at the temple at Jerusalem. The illustration is from the John Brown Bible.

old. Jesus, being in Egypt, escaped the massacre, and the family did not return until Herod was dead, when they settled in Nazareth.

JESUS IN THE TEMPLE

Joseph and Mary visited Jerusalem each year for the Passover. When Jesus was 12 years old, Mary and Joseph were among a group of people returning home after the festival was over, when they realized that Jesus was not with them. They searched among friends and relations but could not find him, so they returned to Jerusalem. At last they discovered Jesus in the temple, questioning the teachers there and discussing religious

matters with them. Everyone who heard him was astonished at the maturity of his understanding. Mary, however, reproached her son and told him how worried they had been, whereupon Jesus replied that they should have known that he had to be about his Father's business.

JESUS'S EARLY MINISTRY
(Matt. 3–4, 14; Luke 1, 3–5)

Jesus did not begin his ministry until he was 30 years old, but it was preceded by the preaching of John the Baptist, who prepared the way for him.

ABOVE: Herod the Great is held in loathing mainly for his pitiless killing of all the male babies in Bethlehem. This *Massacre of the Innocents* from the Scrovegni Chapel, Padua, Italy, is by Giotto (1276–1337).

JOHN THE BAPTIST

Zacharias was a priest, and he and his wife Elisabeth were godly people but elderly and childless. The angel Gabriel appeared to Zacharias and told him that his wife would have a son who would be called John and be a great man of God. Zacharias could not believe that he and Elisabeth could have a child at their age and because of his disbelief he was temporarily made dumb, but his dumbness left him after Elisabeth gave birth to John.

John became a preacher, living an ascetic life in the desert. His message centred on the need for repentance and baptism, and he spoke of a greater one who would come after him. John baptized many people in the River Jordan, including Jesus

himself. At the moment John baptized Jesus, the Holy Spirit descended in the form of a dove and a voice from heaven said, 'Thou art my beloved son. In thee I am well pleased.'

John's uncompromising preaching made him enemies and when he criticized Herod (son of Herod the Great) for marrying his brother's wife Herodias, he was imprisoned. On Herod's birthday, Herodias's daughter Salome came in and danced for him and she pleased her stepfather so much that he promised to give her anything she asked for. After consulting her mother, Salome asked for the head of John the Baptist on a dish. Herod kept his promise and John was beheaded.

JESUS STARTS HIS MINISTRY

After his baptism, Jesus went into the desert and fasted for 40 days and nights. The Devil tempted him, suggesting that if Jesus were God's son he could turn the stones into bread, but Jesus resisted him. The Devil then tempted Jesus with power and wealth, but Jesus resisted him. Jesus was led

ABOVE: One of the few recorded events from the childhood of Jesus – his conversation with the teachers in the temple – is portrayed here by Jacopo Bassano (1517–92).

RIGHT: A mosaic in the dome of the Arian Baptistry in Ravenna, dating from the fifth century AD and depicting the baptism of Christ. The Holy Spirit in the form of a dove descends onto the central figure of Jesus. The figure on the right is certainly John the Baptist, and one assumes that the figure on the left represents God the Father.

to Jerusalem, to the highest point of the temple, where the Devil prompted him to throw himself down to test whether God would save him, but again Jesus managed to resist temptation.

Jesus now began his ministry in Galilee, preaching and healing, and immediately he began to attract crowds, who recognized his gifts and authority. He began to collect a following and called 12 men to be his particular disciples and accompany him everywhere. The first of these were two sets

of brothers, Peter and Andrew and James and John. These four were all fishermen and Jesus called them from their nets and boats to follow him. Another of the disciples, Matthew, was a tax collector. This was a despised profession but Jesus called Matthew from his tax office all the same.

JESUS'S PREACHING AND TEACHING
(Matt. 5–7; Luke 10, 15)

Jesus delivered his message sometimes to individuals, sometimes to the intimate group of his disciples, sometimes to the congregation in a synagogue, sometimes to huge crowds gathered in the open air. The content of his preaching also varied widely, but the main themes were the fatherhood and authority of God and the need for personal righteousness and selfless love. It was mainly

BELOW: This engraving shows the Devil, in a fantastic form, tempting Jesus to turn stones into bread.

with his disciples that he spoke of his role as the Son of God and predicted his own death and resurrection.

Probably the most memorable of Jesus's sermons was the Sermon on the Mount, delivered to his disciples and a large crowd that had gathered to listen. It is a revolutionary sermon, starting with the Beatitudes, where Jesus states that happiness lies, not in wealth, health, or success, but in humility, mercy, peace-making and spiritual hunger. He went on to suggest that anger is as great a sin as murder, and lustful thoughts as bad as adultery. He urged love for one's enemies, disregard for money and possessions, and attention to our own sins, rather than condemnation of the sins of others. He warned his hearers to avoid hypocritical, ostentatious worship and prayer, and taught them the prayer that has come to be known as The Lord's Prayer.

One of the most striking aspects of Jesus's preaching was his habit of conveying his message by means of parables: short allegorical stories of everyday life which illustrated the spiritual points that he wished to make. Many striking parables are related in the Gospels; the best known are probably the stories of the Good Samaritan and the Prodigal Son. The former tells the story of a man who was attacked and robbed by thieves and left wounded on the road. First a priest and then a Levite came along the road and saw him, but both passed by on the other side. Then a Samaritan man came along. Jews and Samaritans were traditionally hostile to each other, but this Samaritan tended the injured man, bound his wounds and paid for him to be cared for at the local inn. The story illustrated the doctrine that we should love our neighbours, and that our neighbour is anyone in need. The parable of the prodigal son illustrates the fatherly love and mercy of God with a story of a young man who leaves home and squanders all his inheritance on riotous living until he is reduced to penury and degradation. When he shamefully returns home he is joyfully welcomed and forgiven by his father.

THE MIRACLES OF JESUS

In his three-year ministry Jesus performed many miracles, the majority of which were concerned with healing of either physical or mental sickness.

ABOVE: This medieval representation of Jesus calling the two fishermen, Andrew and Peter, to discipleship comes from the cathedral at Padua.

The Sea of Galilee, near Tiberias. The Sea of Galilee is actually a large lake, 14 miles long, through which the River Jordan flows. Jesus was a Galilean and the lake is often mentioned in the Gospels. The disciples Peter, Andrew, James and John were called by Jesus from their nets on the Sea of Galilee. The lake and its shores are also the scene of several miracles: the calming of the storm (Matt. 8: 23-27), Jesus walking on the water (Matt. 14: 22–32), and the feeding of the five thousand (Matt. 14: 15–21).

THE GOOD SAMARITAN.

THE PRODIGALS RETURN

He restored sight to the blind, speech to the dumb, and hearing to the deaf (eg, Matt. 9:27–33; 12:22; 20:29–34). He healed people suffering with leprosy, paralysis and epilepsy (eg, Matt. 8:2–3; 9:2–7; 17:14–18). He delivered people from demon possession (eg, Luke 4:33–35; 8:27–35; 11:14). He was able to heal from a distance, without even seeing the sick person (John 4:46–54). On three occasions he raised people from the dead: a widow's son and Jairus's young daughter (Luke 7:11–15; 8:41–42, 49–56); and Lazarus, Jesus's friend, who was raised after having been dead and buried for four days (John 11:1–44).

There were also miracles that involved a supernatural mastery over natural forces. Many of these miracles happened on the sea; the calming of the storm (Matt. 8:23–27), Jesus walking on the water (John 6:19–21), two miraculous catches of fish (Luke 5:1–11; John 21:1–11), the coin found in the fish's mouth (Matt. 17:24–27). Other miracles in

this category include the feeding of the 5,000, when a vast crowd was fed by the multiplication of five loaves and two small fishes (Matt. 14:15–21) and the transformation of water into wine when the drink ran out at a wedding feast at Cana (John 2:1–11).

JESUS'S RELATIONSHIPS

The people who were closest to Jesus once his ministry had started were undoubtedly his disciples, and the men whose relationships with Jesus were the most intimate were apparently Peter, James and John. John is described as 'the disciple whom Jesus loved'. Besides these, there were several women who were close to Jesus, particularly Mary Magdalene, whom he had healed of demon possession, and the two sisters from Bethany,

ABOVE LEFT & RIGHT: Two of the best-known of Jesus's parables are the stories of the Good Samaritan (Luke 10: 30–37) and the Prodigal Son (Luke 15: 11–32). These illustrations of the parables come from an 1816 edition of the popular John Brown Bible, first published in 1778.

THE TEMPEST
MARK IV. 39.

London, Thomas Kelly & Co.

OPPOSITE: Jesus's first miracle was at the wedding in Cana when he transformed water into wine. This early fourteenth-century Byzantine mosaic portrays the miracle.

LEFT: In this illustration from the John Brown Bible, Jesus is shown with his disciples in the midst of the violent tempest which was stilled at his command.

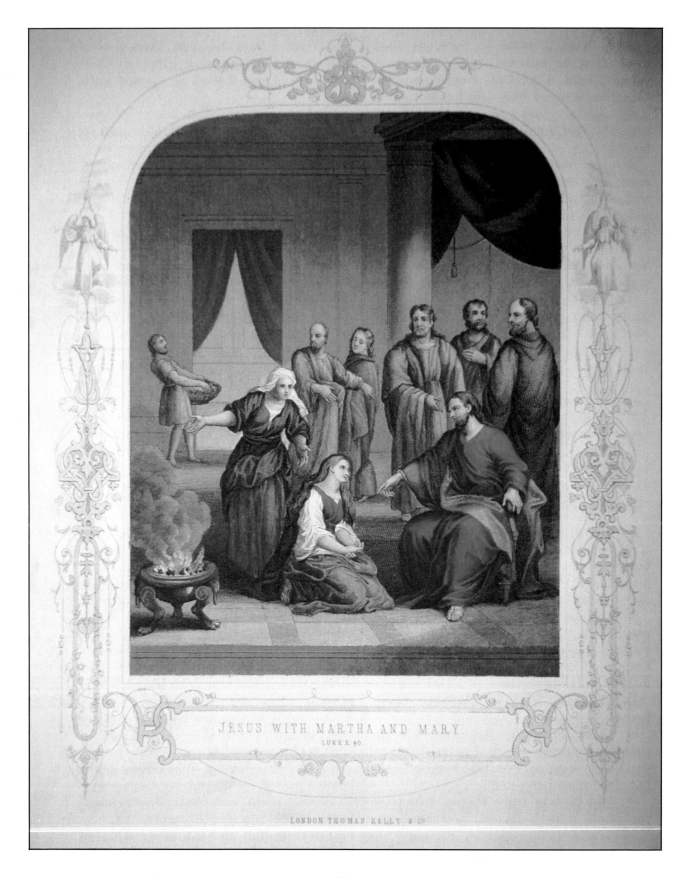

JESUS WITH MARTHA AND MARY.
LUKE X 40.

LONDON THOMAS KELLY & Cº

Martha and Mary, whose brother, Lazarus, was raised from the dead by Jesus. In his attitude towards Mary of Bethany, Jesus demonstrated his disregard for the conventions of the day, when women were not expected to attend to religious teaching. Martha was annoyed when her sister sat at Jesus's feet listening to his teaching, rather than helping with the domestic chores, but Jesus gently rebuked Martha for fussing, and commended Mary's choice (Luke 10:38–42). Jesus's love and compassion for the family at Bethany is shown by his tears over the death of Lazarus (John 11:33–36).

Another example of Jesus's disregard for the conventions of both sex and race is his conversation with a Samaritan woman (John 4:4–26); it was unheard of for a Jewish teacher to speak to a strange woman, and Jews and Samaritans did not mix. His concern for individuals is shown again in his encounter with the notoriously fraudulent tax collector, Zacchaeus (Luke 19:1–10), who climbed a tree to get a better view when Jesus came to Jericho. Jesus called Zacchaeus down and said that he was going to stay at his house, and Zacchaeus repented of his cheating.

Jesus was happier in the company of repentant tax collectors and prostitutes than with the religious leaders and teachers of his day, particularly the strict legalistic sect of Pharisees. He often rebuked them for their hypocrisy, and they constantly sought to catch him out in flouting the

ABOVE: An engraving by Reverdin illustrating the story of Jesus and the tax collector Zacchaeus.

LEFT: This portrayal of the Last Supper is the work of the sixteenth-century Cretan icon-painter Damaskinos.

OPPOSITE: Martha and Mary, the sisters of Lazarus, were two of Jesus's closest friends and his relationship with them is indicative of an unusually accepting attitude to women. He is pictured with the sisters in this illustration from a 1816 edition of the John Brown Bible.

law. This often involved Jesus's attitude to the Sabbath: traditionally this was a day of rest from work, but Jesus thought that healing on the Sabbath was legitimate. The story of the woman taken in adultery (John 8:1–11) illustrates Jesus's conflict with the Pharisees and compassion for individual sinners. The Pharisees had caught an adultress and asked Jesus why she should not be stoned to death, as the law strictly demanded. Jesus's reply was to challenge the Pharisees, 'He that is without sin among you, let him first cast a stone at her', and the woman's accusers one by one went away.

PASSION, DEATH AND RESURRECTION
(Matt. 26–28; Luke 24; John 20–21)

As Jesus's popularity grew, the chief priests and elders saw him as increasingly dangerous and became determined to kill him. Just before the Passover, they met to plot against him. Judas Iscariot, one of the 12 disciples, came to them and agreed to betray his master in exchange for 30 pieces of silver.

THE LAST SUPPER

Jesus and his 12 disciples gathered together in a room in a house in Jerusalem to eat the Passover meal. During this meal Jesus made two predictions. He said that one of them was to betray him and that Peter would deny him three times before the cock crowed next morning.

While they were eating, Jesus broke the bread, gave thanks, and gave it to his disciples, saying, 'Take, eat; this is my body.' Then he gave them the wine to drink, saying, 'This is my blood . . . shed for many for the remission of sins.'

THE ARREST

Jesus went with Peter, James and John to Gethsemane, a garden on the slopes of the Mount of Olives. He was in a state of deep sorrow, and retreated to pray by himself, begging God to take the burden of suffering away from him.

When he returned to the disciples, they had fallen asleep. As he was speaking to them, they saw Judas approaching, with an armed crowd. Judas went up to Jesus and kissed him, as a sign that this was the man that they were to arrest. Jesus was seized and taken to the high priest's house, but his disciples ran away.

Jesus was accused and convicted of blasphemy. Meanwhile, Peter stayed in the courtyard of the high priest's house to see what would happen. As he sat there, one of the high priest's servant girls came up to him and asked if he were one of the men who was with Jesus. Peter denied this and got up to leave, whereupon another servant girl said to some of the men gathered around that Peter had been with Jesus. Peter claimed not to know Jesus, but one of the men insisted that Peter was one of Jesus's friends for his Galilean accent gave him away. Again Peter denied all knowledge of Jesus, and just then the cock crowed.

JESUS AND PILATE

Jesus was taken in chains to the Roman governor, Pontius Pilate, who questioned him, but Jesus remained silent before all the accusations. Pilate was unwilling to interfere in Jewish religious affairs and also his wife had had a dream which warned them to have nothing to do with the death of this innocent man.

It was the custom at Passover for the authorities to release any prisoner of the people's choice, and Pilate thought that he might use this means to release Jesus. However, the priests stirred up the

people to ask for Barabbas, a man imprisoned for sedition and murder. When Pilate offered the people the choice of Jesus or Barabbas, they clamoured to have Barabbas released and Jesus crucified. Pilate then washed his hands to signify his own lack of involvement in Jesus's punishment, and ordered Jesus to be flogged and then crucified.

THE CRUCIFIXION

Pilate's soldiers took Jesus away, stripped and flogged him. They made him a crown of thorns, and mocked him as the King of the Jews. Then they took Jesus out to a place called Golgotha outside Jerusalem, and there he was nailed to a cross.

ABOVE: This engraving of Christ's arrest, showing the treacherous kiss of Judas, is by the Dutch artist Lucas van Leyden (1494–1533).

LEFT: The accused Christ stands before Pontius Pilate in this painting by the Russian artist Nikolai Ge (1831–94).

Jerusalem, showing the Church of the Holy Sepulchre. It is thought by many to be the site of Golgotha, where Jesus was crucified. The Garden Tomb is also claimed by some to be the true site of Christ's crucifixion and burial, but the Holy Sepulchre site is considered more likely, although scholars remain doubtful about both claims. The Church of the Holy Sepulchre is now within the walls of Jerusalem but in Jesus's time the site would have been outside the city.

Two robbers were crucified at the same time, one on each side of Jesus.

At noon, as Jesus hung in agony on the cross, mocked by the crowd, a great darkness fell and lasted for three hours. Then Jesus cried, 'My God, my god, why hast thou forsaken me?'. As he died, the curtain hanging in the temple was torn in two and the land was shaken by an earthquake.

That evening, a man called Joseph from Arimathea, who was a rich man and a disciple of Jesus , went to Pilate and gained permission to take Jesus's body. He took the body, wrapped it in a linen shroud and placed it in a tomb cut into the rock, rolling a large stone across the entrance. The next day, the priests asked Pilate to have the tomb sealed and guarded, for they knew that Jesus had said that he would be raised from the dead, and they feared that the disciples would take his body from the tomb and pretend that he had been raised. The tomb was sealed and soldiers set to guard it.

THE RESURRECTION

On Sunday morning, Mary Magdelene and other women disciples went to the tomb. They found the stone had been rolled away, and the body had disappeared. An angel appeared and told them that Jesus had been raised. They ran to tell the 12 disciples, but the men did not believe their story; how-

ever, Peter and John did visit the tomb and found it empty.

Mary returned to weep outside the empty tomb, when she saw a man whom she took to be a gardener. He asked her why she was crying and she asked him if he knew where the body was. Then the man said, 'Mary', and she knew that it was Jesus himself.

Later that evening Jesus appeared to the disciples and talked to them. One of the 12, Thomas, was not present and when the others told him that they had seen Jesus he said that he refused to believe it until he had personally seen him and touched the nail scars in his hands. A week later Jesus appeared to the disciples again. As soon as he saw Thomas, Jesus invited him to touch his scars.

Thomas answered, 'My Lord and my God!'

Jesus appeared also to two disciples who were travelling to a town called Emmaus near Jerusalem. He joined them as they were talking about the crucifixion and the empty tomb and Jesus explained to them how the Messiah was prophesied to suffer before he came into his glory. However, they did not recognize him until he came into their house to eat with them; as he broke the bread and blessed it they suddenly knew him, but he disappeared.

Jesus appeared again to some of the 12 disciples while they were fishing, and ate with them. Afterwards he took Peter aside and gave him a special charge to look after his Church. For 40 days, Jesus continued to appear to his disciples, after which he was taken up into heaven.

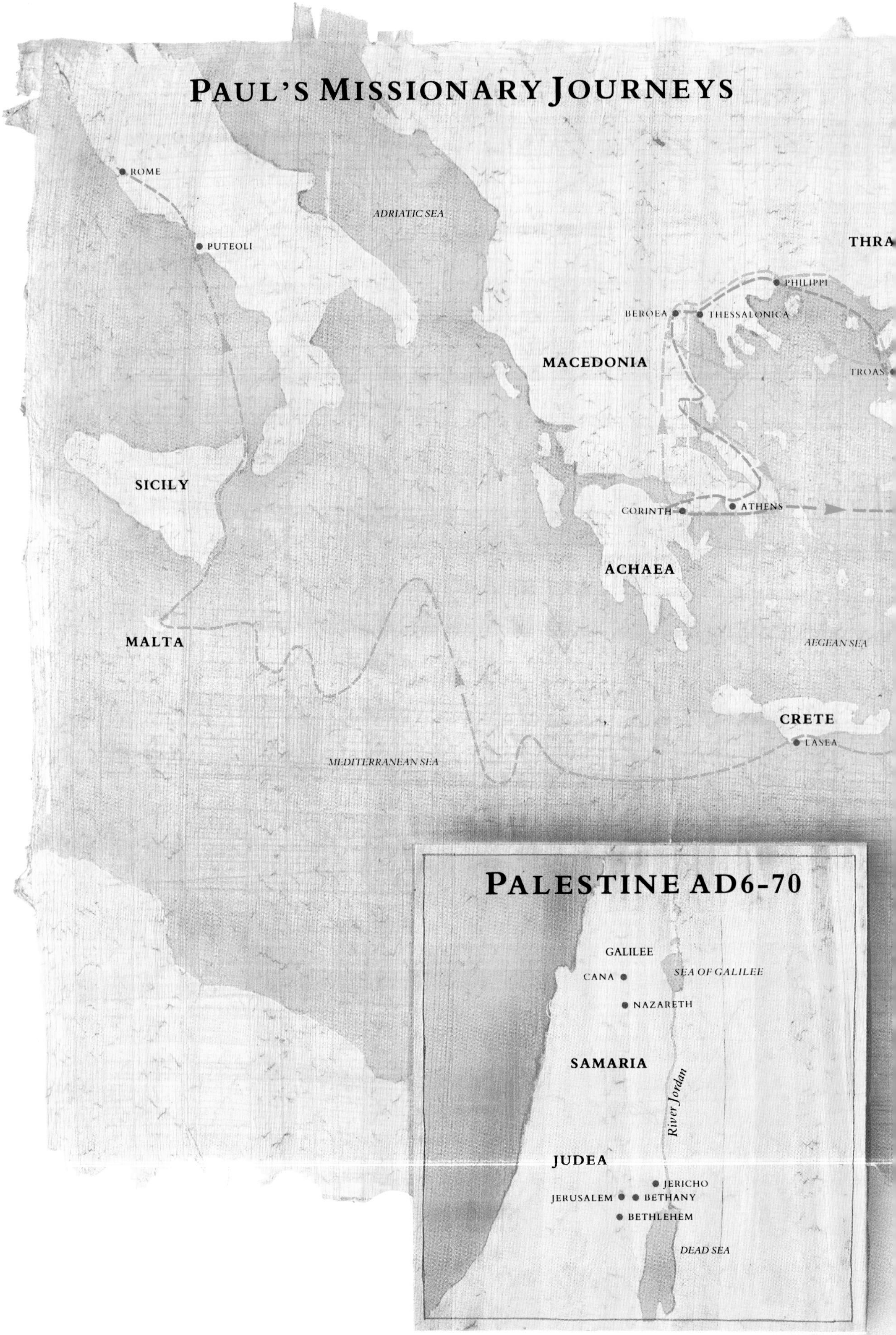

PAUL'S MISSIONARY JOURNEYS

ROME

ADRIATIC SEA

PUTEOLI

THRA

PHILIPPI

BEROEA · THESSALONICA

MACEDONIA

TROAS

SICILY

CORINTH · ATHENS

ACHAEA

AEGEAN SEA

MALTA

CRETE

LASEA

MEDITERRANEAN SEA

PALESTINE AD6-70

GALILEE

CANA · SEA OF GALILEE

NAZARETH

SAMARIA

River Jordan

JUDEA

JERICHO

JERUSALEM · BETHANY

BETHLEHEM

DEAD SEA

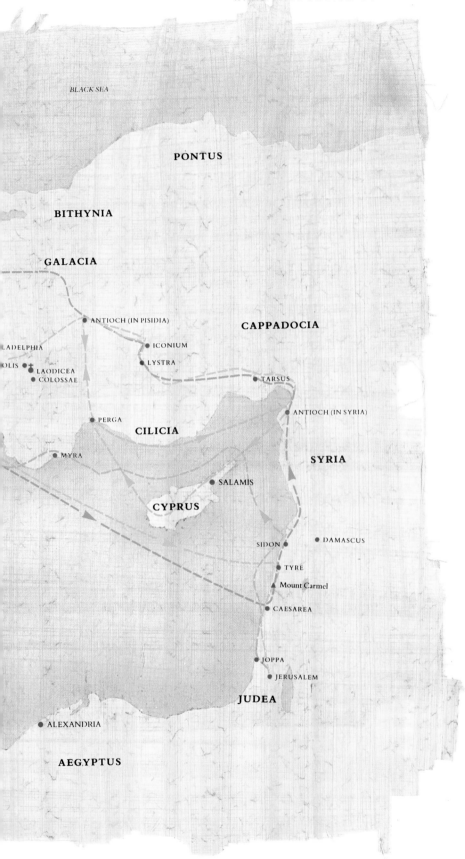

BLACK SEA

PONTUS

BITHYNIA

GALACIA

ANTIOCH (IN PISIDIA)

CAPPADOCIA

LADELPHIA

ICONIUM

OLIS

LYSTRA

LAODICEA
COLOSSAE

TARSUS

PERGA

ANTIOCH (IN SYRIA)

CILICIA

MYRA

SYRIA

SALAMIS

CYPRUS

DAMASCUS

SIDON

TYRE

Mount Carmel

CAESAREA

JOPPA

JERUSALEM

JUDEA

ALEXANDRIA

AEGYPTUS

KEY:

● TOWN/CITY

▲ MOUNTAIN

⚓ 7 CHURCHES OF ASIA

— FIRST
  MISSIONARY
  JOURNEY AD 49–52

— SECOND
  MISSIONARY
  JOURNEY AD 45–49

— THIRD
  MISSIONARY
  JOURNEY AD 53–58

— ARREST AND
  JOURNEY
  TO ROME AD 60

The Early Church

ABOVE: The healing of the lame man at Gate Beautiful
(Acts 3: 1–10). The central figure, lifting the lame man
up, is Peter; John stands on the left.

UR MAIN SOURCE of information on the early Church is the book known as The Acts of the Apostles, or Acts, although we can also learn of the day-to-day running of the churches from the letters of Paul and others.

Acts almost certainly has the same author as the Gospel of Luke and was probably written at the same period. It takes up the narrative from where Luke's Gospel ends, with a style similar to that of the Gospel and the same humanitarian interest. The book tells the history of the early Church with great detail and accuracy, covering a period of some 33 years, from Jesus's Ascension to Paul's imprisonment in Rome.

THE CHURCH AT JERUSALEM
(Acts 1–5)

After Jesus had ascended, a small group of believers began to meet regularly in Jerusalem. The nucleus of this group was formed by the 11 original disciples, plus Matthias, chosen to replace Judas; Jesus's women followers; and Mary, Jesus's mother, and her sons.

THE DAY OF PENTECOST

All the believers gathered together on the day of Pentecost. There was suddenly a noise like that of a strong wind, and it seemed to them as though each one present was touched by tongues of flame. They were all filled with the Holy Spirit – the Spirit that Jesus had promised to send them after his Ascension – and at once they all began to speak in other languages. A crowd gathered, and many foreign Jews thought they heard the believers speaking in their native language. Peter stood up and explained to the crowd that the explanation for this manifestation was an outpouring of the Spirit of God. He preached the gospel to them, explaining that Jesus was the long awaited Messiah, and many of the Jews present believed his message and were baptized. About 3,000 people joined the Jerusalem Church that day.

ANANIAS AND SAPPHIRA

After the coming of the Holy Spirit, the apostles took on new power and authority, both in preaching and in performing miracles, particularly miraculous healings. The Church continued to grow rapidly and the believers met together reg-

ularly to worship; they ate together in each other's houses, and held all their property in common. If any of them were in need, the richer believers would sell some of their goods or property and donate the money received.

One couple named Ananias and Sapphira sold some property in this way, but they decided to keep some of the proceeds for themselves and Ananias handed over only part of the money to the apostles. Peter realized immediately that Ananias was being dishonest and rebuked him, accusing him of lying to God. At that, Ananias fell down dead. Later, Sapphira appeared and Peter asked her if the money her husband had given them was the full amount they had received for their property. She insisted that it was, whereupon Peter said that she would die just as her husband had, and Sapphira, too, dropped dead instantly.

ABOVE: An engraving by Gustave Doré (1832–83) showing Ananias struck down for lying to Peter (Acts 5: 1–6).

ABOVE: *The Stoning of St Stephen*, engraving by William Linton (1812–97). Execution by stoning was the traditional punishment for blasphemy under Jewish law.

DISPERSAL
(Acts 6–12)

The apostles began to attract the hostile attention of the Jewish religious authorities, who imprisoned them, and did all they could to prevent them preaching the gospel. However, they were not deterred, and they continued to draw more and more believers to them.

THE DEATH OF STEPHEN

The apostles had chosen seven deacons to help them in the administrative work of the Church. One of these was Stephen, a man of great faith, who began to gain prominence for his preaching and miracles. After some time he was arrested by the authorities and charged with blasphemy.

When Stephen was charged with speaking against the Jewish Law, he answered with a lengthy sermon, in which he traced God's dealings with his people over centuries, showing how all the patriarchs and prophets blessed by God had been opposed by the people. When he went on to accuse his hearers of rejecting and killing the Messiah they were furious, and their rage increased as Stephen looked up to heaven and described a vision of Jesus at God's right hand. He was seized, taken out of the city and stoned to death. One of the witnesses was a young Pharisee called Saul.

After Stephen's death, the Church at Jerusalem was constantly persecuted, and its members jailed. the result was a dispersal of the believers, many of whom fled Jerusalem but took the gospel message to other areas.

SPREADING THE WORD

Philip, another of the seven chosen as deacons, travelled to Samaria and preached there, also performing miracles of healing. Hearing that Philip was having success in his missionary work, Peter and John joined him in Samaria. Philip had baptized many new believers but none had yet received the Holy Spirit. The apostles began to lay hands on the converts, who then received the Spirit.

There was a man in Samaria called Simon, a magician of skill and some renown. He had been impressed by Philip's message of miracles and had been baptized, but he was even more struck by the result of the apostles' work. He went to Peter and John and offered them money in return for giving him the power to lay hands on people so that they would receive the Holy Spirit. Peter rebuked Simon for believing that spiritual power could be purchased with money.

Philip was now directed by God to travel south, and on his journey he encountered a eunuch who was a high official at the court of the Queen of Ethiopia. He was returning home from Jerusalem and, as he sat in his carriage, he was reading from the book of Isaiah. Philip asked him if he understood what he was reading and the eunuch invited him to sit in his carriage and explain it to him. The passage was Isaiah 53:7–8, and Philip explained that the words applied to Jesus, who had fulfilled all the prophecies about the Messiah. As they continued along the road they came to some water and the eunuch asked if he could be baptized there, on the spot. They stopped the carriage and Philip baptized him.

THE CONVERSION OF SAUL

Saul was a fanatical young Pharisee from Tarsus who had been involved in the execution of Stephen and was zealous in persecuting the Jerusalem believers. He asked the high priest for letters of introduction to the leaders of the synagogues in Damascus, so he could go there and seek out any Christians and arrest them.

As Saul travelled towards Damascus, he was suddenly felled by a blinding light from the sky and he heard a voice saying, 'Saul, why persecutest thou me?' 'Who art thou, Lord?' Saul asked, and the voice told him that it was Jesus. Saul asked what he must do and was told that he must proceed to the city, where he would be told what to do next. When Saul arose, he was blind, and had to be led into Damascus.

ABOVE: Paul fell to the earth when he heard Christ calling to him on the road to Damascus. *The Conversion of St Paul* is by the Italian painter Caravaggio (1571–1610).

Three days later, a Christian in Damascus named Ananias had a message from God telling him to go to a certain street and seek out Saul of Tarsus, who had been blinded and whose sight Ananias would restore. Saul's reputation had preceded him to Damascus and Ananias was very nervous, but he obeyed God and went to the house where Saul was staying. He laid hands on Saul who was then able to see again.

Saul was immediately baptized and, to the amazement of all who knew his reputation and background, began to preach the gospel of Jesus Christ in the synagogues of Damascus. Now he himself became the target of anti-Christian persecution and eventually he had to flee from Damascus. When he returned to Jerusalem and sought out the believers there they were extremely wary of him, but he told them his story and was eventually accepted and began to preach in Jerusalem. Again, he became the subject of death plots, and returned for a while to Tarsus.

PETER'S MINISTRY

Peter travelled widely, preaching and healing. One of his miracles was at Joppa, where he arrived just after a woman believer called Dorcas had died. Peter was taken to the room where her body lay and he prayed for her and commanded her to get up. Dorcas opened her eyes, sat up, and then rose from her bed.

While Peter was in Joppa, he had a vision, where he saw a great sheet descend from heaven, containing all kinds of animals, birds and reptiles. A voice said, 'Rise, Peter; kill and eat'. Peter protested that he had never eaten unclean food, but the voice told him that what God had cleansed was no longer unclean.

Just before this, Cornelius, a Roman centurion from Caesarea had also had a vision. This man, though a gentile, believed in God and performed many acts of charity. In his vision he was told that God was pleased with him and now he was to send servants to Joppa to fetch a man called Peter. Cornelius' men arrived at the house where Peter was staying just after Peter had had his vision. The next day he set off for Caesarea with the messengers and was brought to Cornelius' house. Although Jews were not allowed to visit gentiles, Peter understood from his vision that he was not to regard anyone as unclean, and when Cornelius told him about his own vision Peter was convinced

OPPOSITE: A depiction of St Peter by William Holman Hunt (1827–1910).

BELOW: Peter is released from prison by an angel (Acts 12: 6–8).

RIGHT: An engraving for a family Bible, showing the scene at Lystra when Paul and Barnabas were mistaken for the Greek gods Hermes and Zeus (Acts 14: 6–12).

Engraved for The Revᵈ. Drˢ. Southwell's Family Bible.

The priest of Jupiter would have done sacrifice, &c.
ACTS. XIV. 13.

Corneille pinx.   Royce sculp.

PAUL & BARNABAS reputed as GODS.

that this was what his vision meant. He preached the gospel to Cornelius and his family and friends and, while he was still speaking, his hearers were filled with the Holy Spirit and spoke in tongues. Peter then baptized the whole household.

Peter returned to Jerusalem and reported all that had happened to the believers there, convincing them that the gospel was for the gentiles as well as the Jews. After that, many of the dispersed believers began to convert gentiles, particularly in Antioch in Syria. The Jerusalem Church sent out Barnabas to Antioch to build up the Church, and he was joined there by Saul.

A new wave of persecution began under Herod Agrippa I, and Peter was arrested and jailed. He was woken from sleep in prison by a bright light and the sight of an angel, who led him out of the prison. There was great joy among the believers, but Herod had the prison guards killed.

PAUL'S MINISTRY
(Acts 13–28)

The story of the early Church now becomes dominated by the ministry and missionary journeys of Saul of Tarsus, who is referred to by his Latin name, Paul, from Acts 13:13 onwards.

FIRST MISSIONARY JOURNEY

Paul and Barnabas were sent out by the Church at Antioch in Syria on a missionary tour. They travelled to Cyprus, Antioch in Pisidia, and Iconium, making converts among both Jews and Gentiles. They also made enemies through their preaching, and were forced to flee on several occasions.

In Lystra, Paul healed a lame man and, when the crowds saw this miracle, they went wild, thinking that the gods had descended to them in the form of mortal men. They called Paul Hermes and Barnabas Zeus, and prepared to make sacrifices to them. Paul and Barnabas were horrified and addressed the crowd, protesting that they were just ordinary men, come to turn them from idolatry and towards the true God. Some of the Jews who had opposed Paul and Barnabas in Antioch and Iconium now stirred up the crowd against the apostles, and Paul was stoned.

Eventually Paul and Barnabas returned to Antioch in Syria. Some Judaean believers came there and started to teach that circumcision was necessary for salvation, and Paul and Barnabas were sent to meet with the apostles in Jerusalem to discuss this matter. There were those there who agreed that Gentile converts must be circumcised, but Peter, Paul and Barnabas recounted their experiences among Gentile converts and stood out against circumcision. Finally they reached a compromise by which Gentiles need not be circumcised, but should obey some aspects of the Jewish dietary law.

Paul and Barnabas returned to Antioch but after some time Paul suggested that they return to the towns they had previously visited, to see how the churches they had established were faring. An argument arose between the two apostles, for Barnabas wanted to take Mark, a relation of his who had accompanied them previously, and Paul opposed this because Mark had not stayed with them for the whole trip last time. They could not agree, so finally Barnabas took Mark and went to Cyprus and Paul chose Silas as companion for his next journey.

SECOND MISSIONARY JOURNEY

Paul and Silas travelled to Lystra where they met Timothy, a young man whose mother was a Christian but whose father was Greek. Paul wanted to take Timothy with them so decided to circumcise him to avoid giving offence to local Jews.

They travelled through Phrygia and Galatia but at Troas Paul had a vision of a Macedonian man saying, 'Come over into Macedonia and help us'. So they sailed to Philippi in Macedonia, where they met a woman called Lydia, a Gentile convert to Judaism and a businesswoman who dealt in purple dye. She believed as soon as she heard Paul preach the gospel, and was baptized; she then offered hospitality to Paul and his companions.

In Philippi they came across a slave girl who was possessed by an evil spirit that enabled her to predict the future; she earned a lot of money for her owners by fortune telling. She began following them around, causing a disturbance, until Paul turned round and commanded the evil spirit to leave the girl, which it immediately did. Now the girl had lost her supernatural abilities, and her owners realized that they could no longer exploit these for profit. Furious, they dragged Paul and Silas to the Roman officials, accusing them of being trouble-making Jews who were preaching against Roman customs.

A view of Athens from the Hill of Areopagus. Athens is one of the most important cities of antiquity, and in New Testament times it had become renowned as a cultural and religious centre. The city is named for the goddess Athene, but many other gods and goddesses were worshipped there. The Areopagus is named after Ares, or Mars, the god of war. It was once the meeting place for the Athenian tribunal, and it was there that Paul preached to the Athenians, condemning idolatry and explaining the true nature of God (Acts 17: 15–34).

A statue of the goddess Diana (or Artemis) dating from the second century AD and found in Ephesus, which was the centre of the cult surrounding her. The Temple of Diana at Ephesus was one of the traditional seven wonders of the world. Diana was the daughter of Zeus and goddess of the moon and of hunting. Her cult came to be associated with virginity, but she was originally a fertility goddess and at Ephesus her worship had combined with the worship of a local mother goddess. Note the multiple breasts on the statue, symbolizing fertility. The story of Paul's misadventures at Ephesus (Acts 19: 23–29) reveals that there was a whole industry at Ephesus making money from the worship of Diana.

OPPOSITE: Scenes from the life of Paul on a fourth-century AD diptych in Florence. Paul is seen disputing with philosophers at Athens, bitten by a viper at Malta, and healing the sick on the island (Acts 28: 1–9).

Paul and Silas were beaten and thrown into jail, where they were put into the stocks. That night, as they were praying and singing hymns, an earthquake shook the prison, and everyone's chains fell off and the doors opened. The jailor woke and when he saw what had happened he was about to kill himself, but Paul reassured him that they had not escaped. The jailor took Paul and Silas to his house, tended their wounds and fed them; they preached the gospel to him and he believed and was baptized. The next morning Paul and Silas were released, and returned to Lydia's house.

Paul and Silas travelled to Thessalonica and to Berea, and then to Athens, where Paul was struck by the number of idols in the city. He preached to a large crowd on Mars Hill (the Areopagus), condemning their superstition and idolatry and expounding the nature of the true God. Paul moved on to Corinth and then to Ephesus.

THIRD MISSIONARY JOURNEY

Paul returned to Antioch and then set out again. When he revisited Ephesus, he encountered many involved with the occult who abandoned these practises as a result of Paul's ministry. So many people began to turn to Jesus and away from superstition and idolatry that the silversmiths, who earned their living making models of the goddess Artemis (Diana) and her temple, started to get worried. They stirred up the crowds and started a riot, with everyone shouting 'Great is Diana of the Ephesians!'. Paul left Ephesus.

Paul spent some time in Jerusalem but some of his enemies had him dragged from the temple and arrested. He defended himself before both the Roman and the Jewish authorities, and eventually was sent for trial to the governor, Felix, at Caesarea. Again, Paul defended himself, but the governor kept him in prison, wishing to keep in good standing with the Jews. Felix was succeeded as governor by Festus, who was urged by the Jews of Jerusalem to bring Paul to that city, for they planned to kill him. Paul then appealed to the Emperor, and was brought before Herod Agrippa II and his wife Bernice, who were impressed by him, and allowed him to leave for Rome.

On his way to Rome, a terrible storm blew up and Paul was shipwrecked on the island of Malta, where he performed many miracles of healing. Eventually Paul arrived at Rome where he was kept under house arrest, but allowed to preach.

NEW TESTAMENT LETTERS
AND REVELATION

AFTER THE NARRATIVE books of the Gospels and the book of Acts, the remainder of the New Testament consists of 21 letters (or 'epistles'), addressed sometimes to large groups of churches, sometimes to one church, and sometimes to individuals; and the final book: an account of an apocalyptic revelation.

LETTERS ATTRIBUTED TO PAUL

The letters written by the apostle Paul were all composed from *c*AD 50 to 62, some being written from prison.

ABOVE: The Campo Vaccino, Rome, by Antonio de dipi Joli (1700–77). Babylon was an ancient enemy of the people of God, but the Babylon mentioned in Revelation 17–18 is thought to symbolize the city of Rome, the oppressor of Christ's followers.

The **Letter to the Hebrews**, the primary purpose of which appears to be that of persuading Jewish Christians of the unique claims of Jesus and discouraging them from returning to Judaism, has traditionally been ascribed to Paul, but it is now almost universally agreed to have been written after his death at any time between AD 67 and 90. There is also some doubt about the authorship of **Paul's Letter to the Ephesians**, which some modern scholars believe to be from another author who drew on Paul's letter to the Colossians, and likewise the **Letters to Timothy and Titus**, thought by

some scholars to have been written after Paul's death.

The first nine letters are addressed to the Christian churches which had grown up in particular cities or regions: Rome, Corinth, Galatia, Ephesus, Philippi, Colossae, and Thessalonica. There follows the two **Letters to Timothy** and the **Letter to Titus**, which are known as the 'pastoral epistles', being largely concerned with the care and running of the church. Timothy was Paul's close friend and protégé, and the letters to him contain much of a personal nature. Titus was a pagan convert who had

ABOVE: The temple of Apollo at old Corinth. The old city, destroyed by an earthquake in 1858, was a byword for immorality in Paul's time.

worked closely with Paul and had helped him to establish a church in Crete. The **Letter to Philemon** is a short personal letter written by Paul to a friend, Philemon, living at Colossae. Philemon's slave, Onesimus, had run away from his master and gone to Rome where he had met Paul in prison and became a Christian. Paul eventually sent Onesimus back to Philemon with this letter, asking Philemon not to punish him but to treat him like a brother, for they were now fellow-Christians.

The content of most of the letters is theological, but some of the theology is particularly

119

theoretical, such as in **Paul's Letter to the Romans**, which is largely an exposition of the doctrine of justification by faith. There is also a good deal of warning against false teaching and teachers. Corinth was a town traditionally renowned for its immorality and many of the new believers there were former pagans; Paul wrote to them mainly in order to correct the errors and wrong practices that had arisen in the Church. The Galatian Christians had apparently been led astray by those who taught that Christians must keep to the Jewish Law, and Paul was writing to re-establish his authority and correct these errors. The letters to the Philippians and Colossians also warn against false teachers. The Colossians had apparently been

influenced by some who advocated the worship of angels, and others who advocated excessive asceticism and strict observance of religious rituals. The Thessalonians needed to be put right because some of them had come to believe that the Second Coming was so imminent that there was no need to bother to work. Timothy and Titus are both advised to stand firm against false teaching.

Paul also offers counsel about how Christians should live. He speaks in several of the letters about relationships between husbands and wives, parents and children, masters and servants. Some of this is practical advice, although to the Ephesians he talks mystically about marriage, likening it to Christ's relationship with

BELOW: Rome: the Forum from the Capitoline Hill. Paul's letter to the Romans gives a clear exposition of the doctrine of justification by faith.

the Church. His teaching about the submission of wives to husbands is countered by his message to the Galatians that 'There is neither Jew nor Greek . . . bond nor free . . . male nor female: for ye are all one in Christ Jesus' (Gal. 3:28).

Although there is some overlap in these letters, each makes a unique contribution to Christian thought. Some of the most notable passages are the teaching to the Corinthians on spiritual gifts and the superiority of love, the message to the Galatians on the liberty that the gospel brings, and the stress on reconciliation between Christians in the letter to the Ephesians.

OTHER LETTERS

The Letter from James, addressed to the dispersed Jewish Christians, has been assumed to have been written by James, Jesus's brother, around AD 50, although some scholars maintain that it was written by another James, 40 or 50 years later. The emphasis of the letter is on the ethical behaviour appropriate to Christians, particularly in regard to their attitude to money. James points out the hypocrisy of those who appear to be religious but neglect and oppress the poor, or those who pay respect to the rich and despise poor people. His doctrine is that 'faith without works is dead'.

The Letters from Peter are both attributed to the apostle. The first letter, to Jewish Christians dispersed throughout five provinces, is almost certainly the work of the apostle Peter, and is thought to date from AD 64. The second letter is very unlikely to have been written by the apostle, and probably dates from the second century AD.

In the first letter Peter was writing against a background of persecution of Christians. He exhorts them to faith and godliness and reminds them of the honour and privilege of being among the people of God. He urges them to follow Christ's example in withstanding suffering and false accusations. The second letter contains a denunciation of false prophets and teachers, and a reminder of the certainty of the Second Coming.

ABOVE: Ephesus was the capital of the Roman province of Asia, on the west coast of what is now Asiatic Turkey. It flourished under the Romans in the early centuries AD. The photograph shows a fountain built in the reign of Augustus.

The Letters from John are thought to be addressed to churches around Ephesus. They are all thought to be from the same hand, and very likely by the writer of the Gospel of John. This writer is probably not the apostle, but an associate of his, who was an elder of the Ephesian Church around AD 90.

The first letter reads more like a sermon, and its main theme is an attack on heresy, in particular the heresy being put about by a group of

ABOVE: An early fifteenth-century altar panel showing the Lamb, adored by the elders, and holding the book with seven seals (Rev. 5: 6–14).

false teachers attempting to influence the Church at that time.

Reiterating a theme of John's Gospel, the writer says that God is light, and exhorts his readers to walk in the light and to hate the darkness of sin. He urges Christians to love one another and keep God's commandments. The second letter is addressed to 'the elect lady and her children', but this is thought not to refer to individuals but to a church. John warns again of false teachers, and exhorts Christians to love. The third letter is addressed to Gaius, a church elder, commending him for his adherence to truth and his hospitable habits.

The Letter from Jude, which occupies only one chapter, is usually thought to have been written by Jude or Judas, the brother of Jesus, between AD 70 and 80, although some ascribe it to an unknown author of the second century AD. The primary message is a denunciation of false teaching. Jude uses examples from the Old Testament to show that God's judgment on the wicked is sure and inevitable. He urges his readers to protect themselves against false teaching by building themselves up in faith.

THE REVELATION OF JOHN
This book has traditionally been ascribed to the apostle John. Later scholars thought it more likely to have come from the elder John who also probably wrote the Gospel and the letters of John, but many now think the author was a different person writing near the end of the first century AD.

This book is unlike any other in the Bible. It is a mystical, apocalyptic work, using imagery and symbolism that is difficult for modern readers to interpret. The author, exiled on the island of Patmos, has a vision of the resurrected Jesus, who gives him messages for seven churches in Asia Minor. Individual messages of encouragement or reproof are sent to each church. The following chapters are an account of John's vision, in which he sees: a lamb opening a book with seven seals; four horsemen symbolizing conquest, slaughter, famine, and death; seven trumpets, each preceding a vision; war in heaven between Satan and the angels; and the beast whose number is 666. He then describes a series of plagues and a scarlet woman who, with Babylon, is to be destroyed. The final chapters speak of the millenium – when Satan is bound for a thousand years and Christ prevails – and John's vision of the new Jerusalem. Most of the traditional Christian images of Heaven and Hell derive from John's Revelation.

ABOVE: Satan and the angel which bound him for 1,000 years (Rev. 20: 1–3). The illustration is from the John Brown Bible.

THE NEW TESTAMENT

PALESTINE	REST OF WORLD
300 BC–200 BC	
200–142 BC Judea ruled by the Seleucids; Antiochus III confirms the theocratic status of the Jews	
200 BC–100 BC	
c 130 BC Formation of the Essene community at Qumran	
100 BC–0 BC	**100 BC–0 BC**
63 BC Pompey takes Jerusalem	40 BC ROME: Roman senate names Herod 'King of Judea'
37–4 BC Reign of Herod the Great	27 BC ROME: Octavian is made emperor and named Augustus Caesar
c 7 BC Birth of Jesus	
4 BC – AD 39 Herod Antipas is tetrarch of Galilee and Perea	**0 AD–100 AD**
20 AD–40 AD	AD 14–37 ROME: Emperor Tiberius
c AD 26–36 Pontius Pilate is procurator	AD 37–41 ROME: Emperor Caligula
AD 27 John the Baptist preaching and the beginning of the ministry of Jesus	AD 41–54 ROME: Emperor Claudius
AD 30 Death of Jesus; outpouring of the Spirit of the Church	AD 54–68 ROME: Emperor Nero
AD 34–36 Martyrdom of Stephen; conversion of Paul	
AD 39 Peter in Samaria	
40 AD–60 AD	
AD 45–49 First mission of Paul	
c AD 48 The Council of Jerusalem	
AD 49–52 Second mission of Paul	
AD 53–58 Third mission of Paul	
AD 58–60 Paul held at Caesarea	
60 AD–80 AD	
AD 60 Paul appears before Festus and appeals to Caesar; he starts his voyage to Rome	
AD 64–67 Martyrdom of Peter in Rome	
c AD 67 Paul is beheaded in Rome	

LEFT: An eleventh-century, Anglo-Saxon representation of St Matthew with his Gospel.

125

Index

Picture Credits

The Publishers would like to extend special thanks to David Bloom and would also like to thank the following for their help with this publication and for permission to reproduce copyright material.

Key: *t* = top; *b* = bottom; *l* = left; *r* = right.

7 *l* BIPAC (British-Israel Public Affairs Committee)
  r Israel Museum, Jerusalem
8 C M Dixon (British Museum)
9 C M Dixon (British Museum)
10 Bridgeman Art Library (Bible Society, London)
11 Bible Society, London
12 Quarto Publishing/David Bloom
13 The Warburg Institute, University of London
14 C M Dixon
15 The Warburg Institute, University of London
16 Bridgeman Art Library (Private Collection)
17 Quarto Publishing/David Bloom
18 Quarto Publishing/David Bloom
19 Visual Arts Library (Bodleian Library)
20 The Warburg Institute, University of London
21 Visual Arts Library (Musée des Beaux Arts, Strasbourg)
22 Quarto Publishing/David Bloom
23 *t b* The Warburg Institute, University of London
24 Bridgeman Art Library (British Museum)
25 The Warburg Institute, University of London
26 Mansell Collection
27 C M Dixon (Archaeological Museum, Florence)
28 Fabbri/Bridgeman Art Library (Staatliche Museum zu Berlin)
29 C M Dixon
30 Bridgeman Art Library (Musée des Beaux Arts, Rouen)
31 C M Dixon
34 Visual Arts Library (Indianapolis Museum of Art)
35 Quarto Publishing/David Bloom
36 C M Dixon (Egyptian Museum, Cairo)
37 *t b* The Warburg Institute, University of London
38/9 C M Dixon (Collegiata, San Gimignano, Italy)
40 *t* The Warburg Institute, University of London
  b C M Dixon (Vatican Museum)
41 Visual Arts Library (National Gallery, London)
42 Bridgeman Art Library (Johnny van Haeften Gallery, London)
43 The Warburg Institute, University of London
44/5 C M Dixon
46 Douglas Dickins (Israel Museum, Jerusalem)
47 The Warburg Institute, University of London
50 Quarto Publishing/David Bloom
51 Quarto Publishing/David Bloom
52 C M Dixon (Archaeological Museum, Istanbul)
53 Visual Arts Library (Cincinnati Art Museum)
54 The Warburg Institute, University of London
55 Visual Arts Library (Victoria and Albert Museum, London)
56 Quarto Publishing/David Bloom
57 Bridgeman Art Library (Musée des Beaux Arts, Nantes)
58/9 Bridgeman Art Library (Rafael Valls Gallery, London)
60 C M Dixon (Folkmuseum, Bygdøy)
62 Quarto Publishing/David Bloom
63 The Warburg Institute, University of London
64 Quarto Publishing/David Bloom
65 The Warburg Institute, University of London
66 Quarto Publishing/David Bloom
67 **t** E T Archive (Louvre, Paris)
  b Bridgeman Art Library (Bury Art Gallery & Museum)
68 Bridgeman Art Library (Musée des Beaux Arts, Rouen)
69 *t* The Warburg Institute, University of London
  b Bridgeman Art Library (Château de Versailles)
70 The Warburg Institute, University of London
71 *t* The Warburg Institute, University of London
  b Quarto Publishing/David Bloom
72 C M Dixon
73 Mansell Collection
74 Quarto Publishing/David Bloom

75 Quarto Publishing/David Bloom
76 Lambeth Palace Library
77 C M Dixon
78 *l* Bridgeman Art Library (Agnew & Sons, London)
  r The Warburg Institute, University of London
79 The Warburg Institute, University of London
80 Mansell Collection
81 Bridgeman Art Library (Sunderland Art Galleries)
82 C M Dixon (Louvre, Paris)
83 Quarto Publishing/David Bloom
84 Bridgeman Art Library (Musée des Beaux Arts, Lille)
85 Visual Arts Library (Capodimonte, Naples)
86 Bridgeman Art Library (Prado, Madrid)
87 C M Dixon (Berlin Museum)
88 Quarto Publishing/David Bloom
89 E T Archive (Victoria and Albert Museum, London)
90 *l* Quarto Publishing/David Bloom
  r BIPAC (British-Israel Public Affairs Committee)
91 E T Archive
92 *t* Visual Arts Library (Ashmolean Museum, Oxford)
  b C M Dixon
93 The Warburg Institute, University of London
94 *t* Visual Arts Library
  b C M Dixon
95 *l r* Quarto Publishing/David Bloom
96 Quarto Publishing/David Bloom
97 C M Dixon (St Saviour in Chora, Istanbul)
98 Quarto Publishing/David Bloom
99 *t* The Warburg Institute, University of London
  b C M Dixon
100 The Warburg Institute, University of London
101 Bridgeman Art Library (Tretjakoff-Galerie, Moscow)
102 *t* BIPAC (British-Israel Public Affairs Committee)
  b The Warburg Institute, University of London
103 E T Archive
106 Mansell Collection
107 Mansell Collection
108 Mansell Collection
109 Visual Arts Library (Ste Maria del Popolo, Rome)
110 Mansell Collection
111 Bridgeman Art Library (Private Collection)
112 Mansell Collection
114/5 C M Dixon
116 C M Dixon (Archaeological Museum, Selçuk, Turkey)
117 Mansell Collection
118 Bridgeman Arts Library (Christies, London)
119 C M Dixon
120 C M Dixon
121 C M Dixon
122 C M Dixon
123 Quarto Publishing/David Bloom
125 C M Dixon

Bibliography

Benét, W R, *The Reader's Encyclopedia* (2nd ed., A and C Black, 1965)

Encyclopaedia Britannica (14th ed., 1937)

Illustrated Bible Dictionary (IVP, 1980)

Manser, M H, *Lion Concise Book of Bible Quotations* (Lion, 1982)

Millard, A, *Treasures from Bible Times* (Lion, 1985)

Roberts, J, *Bible Facts* (Dorset Press, 1990; Apple Press, 1990).